PETER ON THE SHORE

vocation in scripture and in real life

"Eternal Father, I offer thee the most precious blood of thy divine Son, Jesus, in union with all the masses being said this day all over the world for the holy souls in purgatory, amen."

PETER ON THE SHORE

vocation in scripture and in real life

Anthony Bannon LC

CIRCLE PRESS
Hamden, CT

Library of Congress Catalog Card Number: 96-83613
ISBN 0-9651601-0-6

©1996 Anthony Bannon LC
Printed in the United States of America
First printing, March 1996
Second printing, September 1997

CIRCLE PRESS
Hamden, Connecticut

*To the man who, on my first visit
to the seminary to see if I had a vocation,
pointed upwards and said, "He's the one
who calls. Ask him, offer yourself to
him," and has never ceased to show
me what it is to be a priest.*

FOREWORD

This book is not meant to be a complete treatise on the abstract matter of vocation. The theology it contains is of a practical nature, and when it gets into theory it is only as an aid towards your responding to God. What God wants to do with your life is too beautiful to bury under a surfeit of theory.

There are many passages of scripture that can enlighten, hearten and warn us about the Lord's call, and there are also common objections that we, our families or our friends come up with as regards vocation. This book is simply a selection of the most typical of both, along with some personal reflections.

You have obviously had some reason to read this far, some reason to pick up the book in the first place—perhaps you are looking for help to make up your own mind, or you want to understand and encourage a relative or friend who feels a vocation. Perhaps you are seeking help to open your heart to accept your son's or daughter's vocation, or maybe you are one of the many members of the Church concerned about the apparent lack of vocations we are suffering, and you want to see if you can do something about it.

Whatever your reasons, I hope that some good comes of your reading. I hope especially that in some way it will give you the means to encourage a new vocation to serve Christ exclusively in total consecration.

It goes to you with my prayers, and remember, if you help even one young man decide to follow Christ as his priest, or one young woman to become his Bride and consecrate her life to him, you will have done something immensely valuable for souls, and beautiful for God.

Every good work that person does during his life will be in a very true sense your good work too.

God bless.

Contents

PART ONE

PART TWO

PETER ON THE SHORE

(LUKE 5:11 THE MORNING AFTER)

*T*HE DARKNESS WAS COOL and a light breeze was already running as the men made their way down to the water's edge.

There was an easy familiarity about the bustle in the darkness, the comforting recognition of patterns made and followed for generations, as well as the stability of other familiar, dependable details.

So much could be recognized in the dark. The limping shadow that could only be Bartholomew, who had been tossed from a horse when he was five years old. Jonah's cough, that through some mysterious habit, lasted only from door to shore. It always stopped when he reached the boat and nobody knew why, least of all Jonah himself. But you could always tell when he came out, and you could always tell when he had reached his boat.

Then there was that other sense that let you pick up Joshua's embarrassment. You didn't see or hear much, but you could tell it as his mother and sister lavished their protection and care. Ever since he had been widowed so young, he had become for them again the baby of the family who needed their care, yet they clung to him so desperately for he was the only support they had. His health and each day's catch was all that stood between them and destitution.

And you couldn't miss the scurrying kids of Philip. While the rest of the town children still slept, these three boys were everywhere. And it would always end in the daily begging to be taken out on the boats, with Philip then patting each one on the head, the taller one and the twins, giving them things to do for mother, chores to help the old rabbi with, and a vague promise of "soon." As he patiently listened to his eldest declare how strong he was now, Philip leaned his shoulder to his boat. The shadow of Simon appeared beside him and crouched to push, too. The three boys added their puny muscles and excited shouts. Simon winked at Philip. "It's almost time for Joseph, you know," he said.

When they were in the water, Joseph called his twin brothers, "OK, now let's get Simon's."

Simon's heart went to his mouth. What was he going to say? What would they think?

"Eh, no—not now."

Curious looks came from the two seven-year-olds and one nine-year-old.

Before the flood of questions started (for Simon was always the first out, Simon had a short temper for anyone who dallied or wasted time or didn't pull his weight, Simon was fun with his fast answers and his arguments with the taxcollecters) he quickly added, "I won't be out today, but I need you boys to help me check the nets in the morning, and I'll teach you some of my special knots."

Curiosity evaporated into excitement, and Simon looked up at the night sky. The fishing was going to be good, he knew.

Most of the boats were on the water. Simon leaned on his on the shore, his beard resting on the backs of his hands, looking out at the familiar activity. A part of him was out there on the water. Yes, the fishing would be good, he knew.

Everything said *"go"* to him. Yet his feet did not move. The slight wavelets lapped around his toes. There was a weight in his heart. There was something happening to him he did not understand.

He spread his hand along the uneven planks. The boat had been his father's before him, but from the age of ten, when his fathers hands began to stiffen, it had been Simon who had scraped, painted, caulked, patched, replaced the dowels, worked the ropes, kept the nets, fixed the mast, patched the sails...

How many surprise storms had they not been through together, this boat and Simon? And that time when he thought the Romans were about to set fire to their whole little fleet...? How many times had he not danced on the prow and you could hear his shrieks of laughter across the water as he pulled in a huge load, especially when John and James couldn't match his eye for where the fish were and Peter let them know it? And then how many times had he not smashed his fist in frustration into its side after hours on the water with nothing to show for it, nothing to bring home?

He ran his hand along the side of the boat.

It was his. It was him. He was a fisher, nothing else. Every chip and dent was part of him. For some reason a line of a psalm shot through his mind: *They put their trust in horses and chariots.* "Am I putting my trust in my boat?" Never had he asked himself that before.

The little flotilla was well out on the water now, with the flap of canvas in the breeze, and Seth's voice as he steered with the oar. Seth always sang. Familiar songs, new songs, nonsense songs, children's songs, working songs. He even knew Greek and Roman songs. And he could imitate any accent. He broke into Matthew the taxcollector's voice as he shouted to Zebedee to be honest and report his whole catch today, and the laughter was immediate. Spirits were high. A wonderful day to fish. Peter half-whispered, "Out a little, then north, that's where they're waiting for you. It'll be a good day."

Distractedly, still leaning on his boat, he played with the small pebbles between his toes, picking them up and tossing them a little, his feelings settling as he heard them plop in the water and send out tiny circular waves. For the first time in years, he was not out there in front, joking, provoking, racing, arguing. ..

But everything had changed yesterday— ironically, with the greatest catch of his career.

He sighed. One last look. There was a hint of first light in the sky.

Even before he turned he felt the two eyes boring through him. She had come to see what would happen, if it was true. Mother-in-law. She understood even less than he. Jesus had cured her once, and the practical woman had immediately gotten up to serve them all. She could understand Jesus helping Simon get a great catch. She did not understand what they told her Jesus had said afterwards: "Leave the boats, you will now catch men." She still remembered the icy stab of fear that had gone through her heart. Simon might just do that! What would become of them?

She had come to see. Now she knew. That Man had got to him. Simon would do it.

In fear and confusion, she swirled away, looking for somewhere to be alone...

Simon saw the gesture. Choked. Perhaps he would have preferred an argument, a tantrum. That silent, pitying and fearful look went to his heart.

He trudged up the beach.

What had happened to him yesterday, as he reveled in the greatest success of his life and the excitement of the crowd that milled around?

He had surely seen the abundance that the prophets had promised would come with the Kingdom of God. All those fish, out of nowhere. Jesus had to be the Messiah. The good times were here, there would be food and peace and freedom. Jesus would do it all. And Jesus had chosen Peter to be with him as he established this Kingdom.

But there were so many other things Jesus said about his Kingdom that did not seem to fit. There would be difficulties. And Simon would have to leave what he loved most.

Fishers of men.

There had been something definitive about the sag of his boat yesterday as he pulled it up on the beach and it settled to one side. Somebody had put a hand on his shoulder at that moment. Had it been John?

And now here he was, shuffling along the deserted beach, his thoughts in turmoil. The other boats far out on the water now. The die had been cast. Peter had stayed. No more fish... Men... What did that mean?

He almost bumped into another beached boat. Two figures alongside it. John and James. The three stood silent.

It sank in. It had happened to all three. Yesterday's words had gone to the very depths of their hearts. "Fishers of men?" *Fishers of men.* Yet, what could it mean?

Not many words were needed between them. For the most part they just looked out to the water and their old life.

Then Peter said, "Guess we better go find him." "Probably at the usual place, he slipped away again last night," said John, unnecessarily. The three of them knew well.

And so, with a last look out to sea, the three turned up the beach, onto the track, and set out.

To find the Master.

Who would make them fishers of men.

SCRIPTURE - *GOD SPEAKS*

Part I

Introduction:
SCRIPTURE AND VOCATION

I f Sacred Scripture is God's word, and vocation is God's
call, his personal word to us, there is obviously a correla-
tion. There is much in Sacred Scripture that will help
us perceive and answer our own call.

creation and call

So much of Sacred Scripture has to do with vocation
because God has done everything by his word. Even going
back to Creation, it seems that he is always calling out. Over
and over he calls things to him. He calls his creatures into existence: there is no light—God calls, and the light becomes present;
there is no order—God calls and things fall into place, each
one where it was meant to be. God creates by calling.

Thus from the outset of scripture we have the
tremendous, commanding (literally), creating, effective voice
of God: *Let there be... Let there be... And it came to pass.* When

it comes time for man, the story is a little different in form, but in fact it is the same. As he breathes life into the clay of the earth it is a powerful command, a call to life, to a participation in his own life.

the drama of wills

And then, just page through Scripture and you will see two wills at work: the divine will and plan, and then the human will which is enmeshed and enslaved in its own plan, dictated by the immediate needs of passions and ambitions—a narrow view that takes it so far from God's path. You will find a summary of this in Psalms 78 and 106.

a call at the service of his will

How does God choose to make his will effective, to get, as it were, his own way?

He does it through chosen people, individuals. When he intervenes directly (Red Sea, plagues in Egypt, miracles of Elijah against prophets of Baal…) it is only to back up the action and message of the one he has chosen to proclaim his message and to do his work.

And this person, though chosen, has to respond freely.

Vocation and response are a single thread that runs through the whole of Scripture. Vocation and response of the people of Israel, vocation and response of individuals.

You can read the whole of Scripture from this angle and God will speak volumes to your soul in the process. You will learn much about him, his ways and yourself. So, independently of whatever ideas I give you in the following pages, you should make the journey through Scripture yourself.

14

What follows are just some of the truths you will find. In each point, I will give you a few quotations which we will comment on. Your own reading will help you discover many more scripture passages related to these. Write them in the margin and make the book your own. Most probably, as you go over these points and read scripture, you will find many more points for reflection. If so, the book will have served its purpose—to get you started.

1. GOD'S ETERNAL PLAN
AKA THE BIG PICTURE
(JEREMIAH 1:5   EPHESIANS 1:3-5)

*B*efore I formed you in the womb I knew you, and **before you were born I consecrated you;** I appointed you a prophet to the nations. (JEREMIAH 1:5).

Now compare that with these passages:

• 2 MACCABEES 7:22 - where a mother speaks to her sons: *I do not know how you came into being in my womb. It was not I who gave you life and breath, nor I who set in order the elements within each of you.*

• *Blessed be the God and Father of our Lord Jesus Christ, who has blessed us in Christ with every spiritual blessing in the heavenly places, just as* **he chose us in Christ before the foundation of the world** *to be holy and blameless before him in love. He destined us for adoption as his children through Jesus Christ, according to the good pleasure of his will…* (EPHESIANS 1:3-5)

an amazing truth

It is worth your while reading over those passages again, letting them sink in. They are God's words and are capable of ushering us into a whole new dimension of thinking and of living. They pluck us out of our earthbound thinking and free us—to enter into the life and dimensions and thought patterns of faith. These could be truly revolutionary words for you, they could turn your world upside down, they could mark a radical change in your life. Once they are accepted in faith.

Let us go back over them to see what they say. But first, let us spare a thought for *who* is saying them. The words from Jeremiah's book are God's. Jeremiah is telling us what God told him when he gave him his calling. So they are words to be taken seriously; they are the real scoop, the source is completely reliable. No guesswork involved. Solid gold. Not to be easily dismissed.

Jeremiah was like so many of us, with his nose stuck in the dust, busy with his own everyday problems, worried about where the next meal was coming from. Then God just burst in on his life.

And how does God explain it?

He does not say: *How is this for a new plan for you I just came up with?* Quite the opposite. He says something that quite simply amazes our human mind: *Before ever you were even conceived in your mother's womb I knew you and I had set you apart for a special mission.* In other words, *the call you are only just perceiving now is not a recent, chance event—**it has always been my idea for you. I never thought of you in any other way.***

Take some time. Go back over that slowly. Take the

thought with you the next time you stop in and visit our Lord in the Eucharist, or go to Mass, or receive Communion.

What God himself is telling us in Scripture is that he gave us life with an appointed task in mind. Our vocation goes back beyond our first encounter with a missionary or priest or sister, and much further back than that first thought of a vocation that wormed its way into our consciousness, that first "maybe" that perhaps shocked us. God's plan, our vocation, has deeper and more mysterious roots than that.

That is why, when asking about a vocation, we often have to change our perspective and point of reference. Some people have "always known" their calling, wanted it from when they were extremely young, but for most it is something that has surprised them—whether by creeping up on them or suddenly popping up out of nowhere. Even in these cases, God tells us that in reality a vocation is something that was in his mind for us, from before we were born.

This means that we cannot sort out or answer our questions about a vocation solely by looking at ourselves or referring to our "experiences." There is another dimension, there is a bigger picture that we have to enter into.

the small picture

It is our nature to look only at the smaller picture.
- Abraham did, and laughed at God's message: *My wife is old and I am advanced in years*; in other words, *What you are asking is impossible.* (GENESIS 17 and 18)
- Moses did: *"I cannot speak"*; in other words, *I am simply not cut out for the mission you are giving me.* (EXODUS 4)
- Jeremiah did: *I am but a child*; in other words, *it's too soon, I*

am not ready yet. (JEREMIAH 1)

- Jonah did: he tried to run away from God; in other words, *Forget your plans, I've got other ideas for myself.* (JONAH)
- Isaiah did: *Alas, Lord Yahweh, I am a man of unclean lips*; in other words, *I am not worthy of what you are calling me to.* (ISAIAH 6)

The smaller picture is the one that our experience and our mind unaided by faith gives us. The small picture is our natural habitat, it doesn't require of us any change or effort. It is immediate, it seems more real to us than any other because it is the fruit of our experience. The smaller picture is what we live and feel and touch and hear and smell, and what we deduce from all of that experience without lifting our heads or our hearts any higher. In it we find our comfort and security.

God's reaction

How does God answer the prophets when they talk back to him, expressing their reservations by referring to their small picture? He says, it is *me* not *you* that has the key to this question. He rebukes them and gives them the big picture, the one we can only get when we look at things from his perspective. He does not retract his command or change the mission to suit their lack of faith.

When Abraham, and then Sarah, laugh at the idea that they will have a child at their age, God asks them: *Is anything too hard for God?* and then he repeats his promise.

God also asks Moses a question, *Who made the tongue?* and then he repeats his order, *Go, I will be with you.*

Jeremiah gets much the same answer: *Go, I will be with you.*

And Jonah fares no differently. God teaches him his lesson, and when the fish has put him on the beach again, God simply repeats his command.

Isaiah has his lips purified and volunteers for the mission.

Is it any different with the apostles and disciples? Scripture does not carry their words of objection, but from some things that Christ said we can suppose that even if they did not express their doubts, they harbored them in their hearts, and our Lord, who reads all that there is in the heart of man, said to them, *When you are dragged before magistrates and judges because you are my followers, be not afraid what you will say on that day. I will put words into your mouths...* Did they learn the lesson the first time around? Well, even after the resurrection we see them locking themselves up for fear of the Jews.

the view from the top

There is another piece of Scripture we should read now that we are on this subject, a truly beautiful passage which will help us greatly in gaining an understanding of God and our vocation. In it, God speaks about the Chosen Nation, but what he says can be applied to each of our souls:

When Israel was a child, I loved him, and I called my son out of Egypt. But the more I called to them, the further they went from me; they have offered sacrifice to the Baals, and set their offerings smoking before idols. I myself taught Ephraim to walk, I took them in my arms; yet they have not understood that I was the one looking after them. I led them with reins of kindness, with leading strings of love. I was like someone who lifts an infant close against his cheek, stooping down to him, I gave him his food. (HOSEA 11:1-4)

Could he possibly have explained in a more beautiful and touching way his care and love for your soul? Can we read these words and then look back over our lives, and not come to the conclusion, and not be deeply moved by it, that God has watched over the life of each one of us with tenderness, compassion, forgiveness, love; undoubtedly with immense hope that we would someday recognize what he was doing and come back to him? That we would someday learn and accept the big picture?

conclusion

In other words, there is a bigger picture as regards your life, and it consists in what God has planned for it, what he has had in mind for you from all eternity. It is what he has been preparing you for and what he is gently leading you towards, insistently, but without forcing you and without destroying your liberty.

It is, basically, what he wants to do through you.

God knows what is in the heart of man. He is not deceived, he has known us always, we are no surprise for Him. He does not go by outward signs. He is not taken unawares by our ups and downs.

Everything that has happened to you that is not fruit of your own evildoing is part of his plan. If you want to know what he wants, look at what he has been doing, read the signs and see what he has been leading up to. Open your heart as well as your mind. Do not be someone who has *eyes* (of faith) *to see yet does not see,* or *ears* (of faith) *to hear and does not listen.*

2. GOD'S SPEECH, GOD'S SILENCE

(1 Kings 9:11-13   Matthew 15:21-28)

L̲et us see how one at least of the prophets experienced God.

Elijah

Elijah was outstanding among the prophets. He carved a huge place for himself in the heart of the people of Israel. He was everything a prophet should be. He was fiery, persevering, fearless in his preaching before a wicked king and queen, victorious in his confrontation with the false prophets of Baal (read 1 Kings 18:17-40 and try to imagine it), without ever losing his human side—after all, he *did* flee in terror of the consequences once he had done the Lord's bidding by standing up to the king and queen; he *did* feel tired and weary and asked God to simply let him die to escape from so much hardship and danger…

Many times we see in the Books of Kings that the word of the Lord was *made known* to Elijah. Often it is not said how. On some occasions we are told it is an angel who comes to him as a messenger, but on one occasion he is sent out to meet the Lord himself. It is a passage well worth our time considering, for there is something to learn from it. This is what we read:

He said, "Go out and stand on the mountain before the Lord, for the Lord is about to pass by." Now there was a great wind, so strong it was splitting mountains and breaking rocks in pieces before the Lord, but the Lord was not in the wind; and after the wind an earthquake, but the Lord was not in the earthquake; and after the earthquake a fire, but the Lord was not in the fire, and after the fire a sound of sheer silence. When Elijah heard it, he wrapped his face in his mantle and went out and stood at the entrance of the cave. Then there came a voice to him that said, "What are you doing here, Elijah?" (1 KINGS 19: 11-13) and there ensues a conversation in which Elijah unburdens himself. He tells God of his zeal for him, how the people have gone astray, and how alone he is and in danger of his life. Then God goes on to give him his marching orders, his mission.

Elijah wrapping his face in his mantle when he goes out to meet the Lord might seem strange to us, somewhat pointless or incongruous, not being the most practical way to see God who was going to pass by. But God was truly "awesome" for the Israelites—they had a heightened awareness of God's majesty, transcendence, and total superiority to man. So much so that *you cannot see the face of God and live.* Out of respect, awe and humility Elijah covers his face. This is how we know it was God himself who came.

This passage definitely tells us something about the experience of God.

There is the shattering earthquake, the hurricane wind that splits rocks, and the consuming fire. Signs of God's power. But they are not him, nor is God in them. Then there comes the utter silence. The prophet recognized the presence of God and he goes out to meet him, face to face.

experiencing God

Elijah's story makes us think a little more critically about what we consider a "religious experience," an "experience of God." When have you really felt God present? When have you experienced God? What makes you say that such and such an experience was "*it?*"

Sometimes we underestimate the value of silence, and we tend to underplay the importance of what happens during it. We expect our experience of God to be a "moving" thing, but it is not always so. Very often it is more like the experience of sheer silence, or a gentle breeze, rather than seismic events. It is in the depth and peace of our inner soul, where deep convictions are born, that we commonly have our experience of him.

This does not mean that it is enough for us to *think* that God has spoken to us for this in fact to be. We can all too easily be led astray by our subjective, inner experiences. Many of these can, as a matter of fact, be more like gales and hurricanes than the gentle breeze or utter silence that the prophet recognized the Lord in. It is in the inner calm of the soul, when grace, God's objective word, the truth of revelation and convictions based on faith (and obedience) are in charge, that we truly experience God.

the value of silence

That silent experience can be more "awesome" than the earthshattering ones. Things can happen to us in silence that would never happen in noise. Indeed, it is often in silence that we test the validity of our crowd-induced and emotional experiences. Don't we often say we need time to think about something? In the face of a high-pressure sales pitch, when we feel we are just getting carried away, don't we look for time out, try to disengage ourselves, so as to think it through?

The fact is, much as we might hate silence, we run to a form of it when there are important things at stake. We trust it much more, and we trust much more what happens within us in silent reflection, than the product of the noise and pressure of external, emotional experiences.

Haven't we, at times, felt remorse for what we did as part of a crowd, once we have had time to be on our own and think about it?

All those who have sought God sincerely down through the centuries and millennia have found the need to disengage in order to speak to him, and especially in order to listen to him. Witness the monasteries and shrines of the most diverse religions, the places of prayer in the deserts, in the remotest mountains, off the beaten paths of the world.

If you want to hear God, silence is a must.

where to find the silence

It might seem like we have to *go somewhere* to find this. But we could say that Christ is much more modern, much more flexible and universal than we might naturally be.

He tells us to find that silence within ourselves, to

make a part of our soul untouched by the world, where we can enter in secret and raise our mind and heart to him, where we can be alone with him.

It is deceptively easy to say but at times not all that easy to do, to retreat from all distraction into the inner room of our "house" (soul), closing the door to the world, and conversing with our Father who knows our every need. But we can safely say that until we get there, to some moments of silence in which we can communicate with him, our grasp of God will be practically non-existent, and we will always be handicapped in our search for him and in our search for answers.

At the same time Christ's approach is a source of hope. It shows us that when we spare a thought for him, he is truly with us; that it is more important for him that we try and raise our mind and heart to him than we *go somewhere* special to do it.

Still, it is always easier to enter into that interior silence when we seek outside circumstances that help us, such as seeking time on your own in a church. Drop in, make visits before or after classes, or at a lunch break, or on the way home from work. Make silent time for prayer alone at home before the day begins, or when evening falls.

the fruits of silence

Read on your own what happened to Elijah after he had encountered God in silence.

When God gives the prophet his marching orders and outlines his mission, it is not a message of consolation. God does not cut back on the sacrifice he will ask of him. There is no concession to the prophet's fears. God sends him right back to do certain things that were bound to make powerful people's blood boil (anoint new kings, anoint another prophet to continue his own work).

Often we make the mistake of praying in the hope that we will be relieved of responsibilities, that we will somehow be excused from the battle. It is not unusual for us to be disheartened by the experience of dryness in prayer, forgetting that it is just another form of God's silence and that we should find him there too. We find it very tempting to seek and bask in experiences that are, to varying degrees emotional, letting them displace from our consideration the more troublesome aspects of following God. Such as standing up for our principles. Such as giving him the first shot at our lives.

To have the strength to do that, we need the true experience of God in the silence and calm that characterize him. Out of this silence and communion with God are born the deep convictions that carry us through life.

another type of silence

The Canaanite woman (MATTHEW 15:21-28) experienced a different kind of silence, more like the silence that we have mentioned above regarding dryness in prayer.

She came to Jesus with a petition but she gets no acknowledgement and no answer. It must have lasted a while, and it seems that the disciples tried a cease-and-desist order but she didn't heed them. They appear at the end of their wits as they turn to him and ask him to send her away *because she is crying* (shouting) *after us*.

Then she gets a treatment from him that seems even worse than silence. She gets what looks like a refusal: *I was sent only to the lost sheep of Israel.* Doesn't it remind you of the answer Mary got at Cana, *What is it to me and to you?*

But both Mary and the Canaanite woman grew in their experience of God's silence. For Mary, Christ's silence, the apparent disappearance of his divinity for so many years in Nazareth, must have been near unbearable—at least it was definitely in stark contrast to her experience at his birth, with the angels and shepherds and wise men. But both had grasped the mystery of his love. In that dryness both had grown in their faith and in their absolute trust.

So when the Canaanite woman gets what seems like an insult added to the refusal (*It is not fair to take the bread of the children and give it to the dogs*) she does not give up. She recognizes herself in the comparison, accepts the truth that she has no right to what she is asking for and yet does so anyway.

Christ's reaction is even more instructive. He praises her for her faith. But that faith is the gift he has given her as she prayed and as he tested her. She accepted his gift and used it.

conclusion

So out of God's silence is born the faith that can move mountains.

As you ask God for answers regarding his plans for you, do not give up. Seek silence yourself in order to speak to him and listen as well. Accept his silence and don't expect an emotional high every time you go on your knees. Ask him especially to increase your faith and make you strong to accept his way.

3. TELLING GOD'S CALL FROM MY IMAGINATION
(LUKE 14: 28-32   LUKE 18:9-14   ACTS 9)

We are faced with a very real and worrying problem: if God speaks in the privacy of my heart, and if a vocation is such an intensely personal thing, how can I tell if what I feel is not just my feverish imagination, my oversensitivity at work, making me think it is God?

There are a few pieces of the New Testament that we can look at together and which might help: Luke 18:9-14, Acts 9, Luke 14:28-32.

figments of our imagination

Christ was anxious for his followers not to be led astray by the common errors to which our human nature is exposed. He noticed how some people lived in their own world, so to say, when it came to religious things. They lived in a dream world, thinking they were righteous when in fact they were not; and because they thought so, they looked down on others that they thought were not, calling them sinners and treating them with contempt.

When he saw this he told them a parable, the one we call *The Pharisee and the Publican*. You are familiar with it, but to refresh your memory, take St. Luke's gospel and read chapter 18:9-14.

The story is quite vivid and extremely easy to imagine, it is a perfect vignette of human nature as we know it from experience.

Two men go up to the temple to pray. One of them is full of himself, and as he stands there proudly his prayer consists in telling God how great he (the man who is praying) is. Just to prove it, he not only reams off his great and wonderful fastings and fulfillment of the various intricacies of the law, but also in the process he compares himself with others that in his opinion are not nearly as good—the sinners, the dregs of humanity, worthy only of contempt. But he is holy. God would do well to realize what a prize he has in him.

Meanwhile the other man almost hides himself, he does not dare to come very close or even look up to heaven. All he does is beat his breast and ask God for mercy, for he knows he is a sinner.

According to Christ this second man went down to his house justified while the first did not. Here we have food for thought: the "expert" was wrong.

the Pharisee

The pharisees were the experts in Israel as regards fulfillment of the law. They were the holy ones, and their name means "the separated ones." In other words, their striving for justice and holiness separated them from the run-of-the-mill Jew.

It was not easy to be a pharisee, it entailed fasting and prayer and a scrupulous fidelity to countless laws and their application. It was involved and arduous.

It was quite understandable that any man doing all those things would think himself superior to others. It is quite to be expected that a man making such sustained effort and going to such extremes would want some recognition and respect. He would want to feel it was worthwhile and that all of this bother he was undertaking was really making him a better, holier, more perfect man. So he would make sure that people saw him pray, that they saw him give alms, that they noticed on his face that he was fasting, that they saw and admired and gazed in awe at his meticulous religiosity. And it seemed that he began to think that it was somehow only right that God too should gaze in awe and gratitude at such a wonderful servant, the pride of Israel.

Now it is sobering to realize that what he thought was bringing him close to God, justifying him, was in reality taking him in the opposite direction. It was separating him not from sinners as he thought, but from the God he thought he was honoring.

In other words, he was mistaken. He was mixing up his subjective ideas and feelings—for which he had much supporting evidence—with God's view. He thought God must see things exactly as he did, he must surely know what a just and righteous man he was.

This is a fundamental error and we can all make it. No, we all *do* make it. Over and over again.

We get some idea into our heads, and we figure God must see things exactly as we do. It does not follow. Our hang-ups and obsessions can make us focus on the wrong things. Just as Christ said about the pharisees in a colorful exaggeration, we strain out the gnats and then go ahead and swallow entire camels instead. The pharisees went to great lengths to define what was *work* so as not to do it on the Sabbath (they wondered if carrying the extra weight on their feet when wearing sandals constituted *work*, so as to know if they could wear sandals or not on the Sabbath) and thus avoid breaking the law, yet, as Christ said, in the process they forgot about the essence of the law which was mercy (*I want mercy and not sacrifice,* he quoted back to them from the Old Testament).

consequences

Does this have much to do with vocation? Well, yes, it has a lot to do with the thought process that goes into a vocation, and with any time we try to figure out what God is really saying.

The lesson from this piece of gospel is that we are always in danger of thinking about things in a very subjective way, of fabricating our own remedies and truths which can at times be very mistaken. Just the fact that we think something, and are very sincere about it, does not make it correct. The pharisee was thoroughly convinced that he was right, that he was better than the publican, yet he was not. The pharisee thought he left the Temple justified, holy, in contrast with the publican—yet Christ tells us that things were very different. It really was the publican who was justified.

The whole point of the story is that we can easily be led astray by our pride, thinking we have everything figured out for ourselves, while in reality the only way we can be free of the dangers involved is humility, to recognize that we do not have the answer in ourselves, to go to God and ask him, and to accept what he says.

Somebody else, with experience of God's ways, has to help us discern if it is he who is calling. It is something we cannot figure out just on our own.

outside help

Let us take a look at what happened to St. Paul and how he found the meaning of it. (ACTS, chapter 9)

Saul (Paul's name at the time all of this happened) was a persecutor of the Church. Mind you, not any mild critic or your regular two-bit harasser. Saul of Tarsus breathed fire. He breathed threats and murder against the disciples of the Lord. People trembled at his name. But he did everything legally—he got the warrants, and then came down heavy. He put men, and women too, in chains and brought them to Jerusalem. Here was no enemy of the death penalty. There was no way anyone could escape his zeal.

It was on one of these missions as Saul, still breathing threats and murder, headed out to Damascus to take Christians prisoner, that God's time came. As he rode, a great flash of light enveloped him, he was thrown to the ground, and he heard a voice. It was Jesus who asked him why he was persecuting him.

Now this would seem to be the perfect moment for Christ to explain everything to Saul. He certainly had his attention. But Christ's words seem strange to us under the circumstances. Instead of pressing his advantage he says to Saul: "Get up and enter the city, and *you will be told what you are to do.*" Saul doesn't object. He gets up and does as he has been told. He has the added bitter surprise that he has now become blind. What a humiliation for this fiery self-starter, to have to be led around by the hand. As a soldier who knew he was feared he must have felt very vulnerable.

Saul does not know what lies ahead. He is at a loss, so he obeys. He waits. He fasts. We can be sure he prays. But he does not expect any other answer to his prayers than to be told by someone what he was to do.

That someone—his name was Ananias—was being approached by Christ in a vision, and was having a problem with what he was being asked to do, for the Lord was telling him to go and visit Saul. Ananias knew only of the ill-gotten fame of Saul as a persecutor, and it made going to see him a most dangerous and undesirable task—so, quite naturally, he objects by reminding Christ who the man is they are dealing with. But Christ insists. Ananias goes, perhaps thinking his own time has come.

When Ananias goes in and delivers a simple message to Saul—*The Lord Jesus who appeared to you on your way here, has sent me so that you may regain your sight and be filled with the Holy Spirit*—the New Testament says that *immediately something like scales fell from his eyes, and his sight was restored.*

Saul regained his physical sight. But some spiritual "scales" fell from the eyes of his soul as well. He got up and was baptized, and now by faith he saw that Jesus was the Son of God. His soul acquired a new spiritual sight.

This is significant for us. What gave Paul the gift of faith was not the vision on the roadside, although God could have given it to him there. The gift came through the man sent by Christ, who explained the meaning of what had happened on the roadside and who gave him the sacrament of baptism.

Even Paul needed someone to help him understand his experience.

using our own heads too

There is a further piece of the gospel we should keep in mind when we are trying to figure if what we are feeling and thinking is from our imagination or from God, and it is some advice Christ gave his disciples after he had spoken to them about the sacrifices they would have to make to be his followers.

He tells them to think seriously and realistically about it. He tells them to give at least as serious and practical thought to it as they would to a construction job or to a military undertaking... *for which of you, intending to build a tower does not first sit down and calculate the cost, to see whether he has enough to complete it? Otherwise when he has laid a foundation and is not able to finish, all who see it will begin to ridicule him saying, "This fellow began to build and was not able to finish." Or what king, going out to wage war against another, will not sit down first and calculate whether he is able with ten thousand to oppose the one who comes against him with twenty? If he cannot, when the other is still far away, he sends a delegation and asks for terms of peace.* (LUKE 14:28-32)

But to understand this passage well, we have to add the other that says, *With men this is impossible, but with God all things are possible.* (MATTHEW 19:26) With Christ it is never a question of mere human numbers and calculations, for the realism of the gospel is a realism that does not function independently of our faith. We should think ahead, make our calculations, figure out if what we propose is feasible—but all the while we should never think as man thinks but as

God thinks. God's grace should be an essential element we take into account in our discernment.

conclusion

From all the above it is clear that you have to seek the help of a spiritual director at some stage of your search. He must be someone you can trust, and very often the sign of this is that he is not afraid to tell you things you sometimes do not want to hear.

Principally he has to tell you if you are losing touch, either with reality or, on the contrary, with your faith, as you search for God's will in your life.

4. THE MYSTERIOUS WAY OF PRAYER

(LUKE 11:1-13 ISAIAH 6:1-9)

Sad to say, but in real life it seems that we do not often experience the fruits of prayer as Jesus explained them to us—that everyone who asks, receives and everyone who searches, finds and for everyone who knocks, the door will be opened. (LUKE 11:10) *How long have I searched*, we at times feel like saying, *and have not yet found the answer to my vocational questions?*

And still they tell us to pray about a vocation!

How come? And, how?

prayer

Prayer is at the core of our relationship with Christ and in some way it sums up and reflects the type of Christian life we are living. I mean, that by looking at the quality of our prayer we can tell what kind of Christians we are. We can also take from the ideals we have in the Christian life an example of how to pray.

That may sound abstract, so let us see an example, the best example possible. Let us take a look at how our Lord told us to pray in order to learn once more some important things. You will find the Lord's prayer in Luke's gospel, at the beginning of chapter 11 and in Matthew's, a little into chapter 6.

the law of the Kingdom and the law of the Prayer

But, just to confuse you, let us start somewhere else!— by stitching together several things Christ said and which you will recognize: *if you try to save your own life you will lose it, but if you lose your life for the Kingdom you will find it; the first shall be last and the last first; he who humbles himself will be exalted and he who exalts himself will be humbled; seek first the Kingdom of Heaven and all the rest will be given you.*

There is an unusual *law* at work in the Kingdom of Christ, a law that is diametrically opposed to the world and its ways, and which is incomprehensible to the world. It is the law that was summarized by Christ when he said that he came not to be served but to serve.

the Lord's Prayer

When the disciples wanted to pray but didn't know *how*, they asked Christ, and he gave them the *Our Father* as the model of all prayer. So, what answer does the *Lord's Prayer* give to our question as regards praying about a vocation?

In it, Christ teaches that our first thoughts in prayer should be not for ourselves but for God himself and his things. So he opens with an invocation, *Our Father who art in heaven*, and a desire/petition in which the "beneficiary" is God himself, *hallowed be thy name*; followed by another, *thy King-*

dom come, and yet another, *thy will be done on earth as it is in heaven*, which are all centered on the Father.

Only then does he move on to things to ask for ourselves, *give us this day our daily bread*—note that it is something basic that is asked for, something simple, straightforward and necessary to life—which is followed by, *and forgive us our trespasses as we forgive those who trespass against us*—which commits us to behaving as we wish to be treated—and finally, *lead us not into temptation but deliver us from evil*—which again is directed towards us doing God's will in our lives.

From our Lord's example and instruction we see that real prayer is truly a God-centered endeavor. It cannot be self-centered, any more than our faith can be self-centered rather than God-centered.

It is worth pausing and comparing how we pray with how Christ wishes and teaches us to pray. The comparison may lead us to some very helpful discoveries about ourselves and our priorities. No doubt it will also shed some light on the reasons for the fruit, or lack thereof, in our prayer.

vocation and prayer

I believe there are fundamentally two ways to pray about a vocation. One is good, the other is much better.

The first way is to ask God for light. *Lord, show me what my vocation is.* And then we go looking for signs. We do not want to make a mistake. And so there is also some worry as we pray, *Is this right? Is this the best for me?*, etc. What we want to know, and basically what we search for through our prayer, is what God wants of and for us. There is a lot of merit to this. But while through this process, yes, we are going to God, there is still a lot of thought there for ourselves. To a great degree we are still the center of our thought and concerns.

The second way is to take the *Our Father*, Jesus' advice for prayer, and make it our model even as we seek our vocation. The radical difference here is that the focus is no longer on ourselves. The center of consideration is entirely God, and entirely his Kingdom.

The *Our Father* is a tremendously committing prayer, and if we prayed it with utter sincerity it would unleash a spiritual power and fill our lives with God in such a way that the face of the earth would certainly be changed and renewed. The gospel would sweep through the world.

Following the *Lord's Prayer* and what we called the *laws of the Kingdom* above, let us see how we can improve (and thus make more effective) our prayer regarding a vocation.

real prayer

Firstly, let us not seek ourselves in prayer. *Hallowed be* thy *name,* Thy *Kingdom come.* But these are not passive petitions. We cannot pray them and then sit back waiting to see what happens.

So, secondly, we must pray *with our loins girt,* and ready to work. We cannot expect to say the words and then in some mysterious way think that the fruits are going to come down from heaven. *Not everyone who says Lord, Lord, but those who do my Father's will...* To pray those petitions of the *Our Father* is the same as to pledge to God, *I am going to praise and honor your name—I am going to do all I can to make your Kingdom come.*

St. James says something in his letter about works of charity that is applicable here. He was writing to some

Christians who thought they had faith but who did not have works, and he said to them...*If a brother or sister is naked and lacks daily food, and one of you says to him, "go in peace, keep warm and eat your fill" and yet you do not supply their bodily needs, what is the good of that? So faith by itself, if it has no works, is dead."* (JAMES 2:15-17)

We could say that similarly, prayer without action is dead. Dead trees don't bear fruit. Neither does dead prayer.

Prayer without willingness to act is not much better than hypocrisy. There could be nothing emptier.

Willingness for action is the willingness to pay the price for the Kingdom to come. As someone has said, the only way to pray that part of the *Our Father* is with your sleeves rolled up.

This means we must to be willing to share in Christ's cross, because it was through the cross that he inaugurated the Kingdom. Thomas the apostle sounds a little fatalistic to us when he says, *"Let's go up to Jerusalem and die with him"*—that was when Jesus was not heeding their warnings and made it obvious he intended to go there despite the danger signs. However, his and the other apostles' attitude towards the cross changed with the experience of Christ's resurrection. Our acceptance of the cross should not be fatalistic and mere resignation as St. Thomas' first reaction was. It should be full of hope and enthusiasm. "Hail, oh Cross, our only hope."

Our prayer should also be a pledge not to leave Christ alone in his love for humanity and in his work of salvation. This is not presumption. It is Christ himself who has asked for workers for the harvest, Christ himself who sent the apostles to preach and baptize. We do not go *instead of* him, but *with* him and *as* him, *Whoever receives you receives me, and whoever receives me receives the One who sent me.* Perhaps the ultimate mystery of Christ is his unselfishness in making us partakers of his work, of having us take part in the redemption of our brothers and sisters, making up for the part we often play in leading them astray. Christ's pardon not only forgives us this, but allows us humans to rebuild through him, with him and in him what we have destroyed.

praying about a vocation

The above leads us to see that while we should pray about a vocation we should make sure we do it well, by praying with the proper attitudes. We should seek the silence of prayer in order to sort out our impressions, to let them sink in, to give God a chance to really speak to our soul.

To pray about a vocation is not merely to think about it in the silence we associate with prayer. To pray about a vocation is to ask for light and to ask for understanding, certainly. But it is most important to pay attention to the attitude with which we pray, and we should also ask God to improve our attitude, so as to acquire complete willingness to accept whatever answer he gives us.

When we are ready to accept the answer we are most likely to see it when it comes. When we are still struggling with our attitudes we are inclined to ask God for more proofs than those he is already giving us.

praying for a vocation–Isaiah

This takes us one step further than praying about a vocation. Is it right to do this?

Then I heard the voice of the Lord saying, "Whom shall I send? Who shall be our messenger?" I answered, "Here I am, send me." (ISAIAH 6:8)

You have to take this passage in its context in order to understand it:

Isaiah is in prayer. He is favored with a vision of the Lord Yahweh seated on a throne in all his majesty, attended by angels. In the face of this majesty and power he experiences his own smallness and above all, his own wretchedness and sinfulness, and when he cries out his confession an angel approaches and purifies him of his sin and iniquity. Thereupon he hears the Lord speaking, asking who could be his messenger. And Isaiah volunteers.

Several things you should note.

Firstly, the prophet was in prayer. Secondly, his prayer was an extraordinary experience of God. Thirdly, his experience of God gave him a new, humbling experience of himself—he realized what a sinner he was and how unworthy he was to be in God's presence. Fourthly, this realization made him cry out, and God takes the initiative to purify him by sending him his angel to do so. Finally, *once he is purified, he enters into a whole new dimension in his relationship with God.*

In this new relationship he no longer feels the need to run away and hide from God. He is drawn into God's reflections and plan. He sees and hears what God wants. And he volunteers. Blindly. Note that is only *after* he has volunteered that he is told what God wants him to do and say. He had signed a blank check over to God.

He offered himself. He asked God to send him. This was much more than asking God if he was being called. It is very different to say, *Lord, are you thinking of sending me?*, than to say simply, *Lord, send me.*

praying for others

It is a good thing to pray for others. But sometimes we do a good thing badly.

There is the danger of praying with the spirit of the pharisee who gave thanks to God because he was not like other men. We can pray for the needs of others with the detachment of someone who is asking for others what he does not need himself (in other words with a sense of superiority, forgetting that even the good attitudes we have are a gift from God). So we should pray with humility, recognizing that the first person to need what we are asking for others is ourself.

There is also the danger of praying without commitment—as if we had nothing to do with what we are praying for coming about. We ask God to help someone, and that's it. Contrast this with St. Francis' prayer. Instead of praying just for peace to come, he said:

"Lord, make me an instrument of your peace. Where there is darkness *let me bring* your light; where there is despair *let me bring* your hope…"

We should pray with this same attitude. When a brother or sister has a need we should pray for them, but we should also pray that we will have the generosity to be part of the answer to that prayer if possible. There will, of course, still be things that it seems you can do nothing about beyond asking God to grant them. Nevertheless you should always say, "If there is anything I can do, any sacrifice I can make to help this come about…"

suggestions

Maybe you could shift the emphasis of your prayer.

Maybe what your prayer needs in order to be more generous is the purification that confession gives.

Maybe in your prayer you should take to God the needs and miseries you see in the world around you.

Maybe then in your soul you will hear him asking, *Yes, they need to hear the gospel preached, they need to have their sins forgiven, they need to be nourished on the Eucharist, they need to have someone show them my love and charity, but how? Whom shall I send?*

Maybe then the Holy Spirit will move you from a prayer of intercession to a prayer of offering, and you will find yourself saying, *Lord, send me.*

5. MOTHER, FATHER, BROTHERS, SISTERS

(LUKE 14:25-27 MATTHEW 10:37-40)

These are some of those words that we often wish Christ had not said.

Whenever we read them we almost wait to see if our Lord will have second thoughts and hurriedly backtrack, apologizing and saying that it is just a figure of speech, or that he just got carried away on the tide of his own passionate rhetoric. At times we might find ourselves embarrassed to read them in public, and simply mutter in our hearts, *This is a hard saying.*

But when we dare to look up at Christ, we do not find him embarrassed at what he has let slip out, nor do we find him rushing to take his words back, or to rephrase and water them down.

He just looks at us and says, *"Because of this, will you also go away?"* (cfr. JOHN 6)

Let us read the actual words of the gospel:

Now great multitudes accompanied him; and he turned and said to them, "If any one comes to me and does not hate his own father and mother and wife and children and brothers and sisters, yes, and even his own life he cannot be my disciple. Whoever does not bear his own cross and come after me, cannot be my disciple." (LUKE 14:25-27)

The first thing we notice here is that Jesus is not speaking in private, in one of those many closed sessions he often had alone with his twelve apostles. He is addressing the great multitudes. And further, the specific reference to family members seems unprovoked in the context. It is not as if someone has just said to him, *I will follow you if my family will only let me,* to which he answers by putting the family in its place—much in the same way as he declared the hindrance of riches when the rich young man turned away from him in sadness because he was not willing to give up his possessions (cfr LUKE 18:18-25).

So here, he is not specifically addressing an isolated instance of overcoming the opposition of parents and siblings. Jesus is laying down a general principle, valid for all times and circumstances, and not only for when there is opposition. He is not saying: *If family members are a problem then you have to put them in second place.* He is saying: *If right off the bat you do not put your blood relationships in second place you are simply not worthy of me.*

He even goes further than that to say something that affects us even more directly and personally (and perhaps will make your family feel a little better about the place you are assigning them): *If you do not put yourself, your own life, in a lower place than me you are not worthy of me: if you do not take up your cross daily and follow me you are not worthy of me.*

In other words, Christ is establishing a principle and a pattern: we are only worthy of him when he is everything to us, and when we embrace his cross.

Do not think that I have come to bring peace on earth; I have not come to bring peace but a sword. For I have come to set a man against his father, and a daughter against her mother, and a daughter-in-law against her mother-in-law; and a man's foes will be those of his own household. He who loves father or mother more than me is not worthy of me; and he who loves son or daughter more than me is not worthy of me; and he who does not take up his cross and follow me is not worthy of me. He who finds his life will lose it , and he who loses his life for my sake will find it. (MATTHEW 10:34-39)

Many people find this passage scandalous and confusing. Isn't Christ the *Prince of Peace*? Didn't the angels announce and sing *Peace on Earth* at his birth? So how come this contradiction? Doesn't he want us to be happy? Isn't Christian living a thing of joy, of resurrection? Then how come these dire predictions?

To have some chance of understanding what Christ says here we have to go back to the core of his message in the Beatitudes.

In the Beatitudes (you'll find them in Matthew 5:1-12) we have Christ's formula for happiness, and reading them leaves us in no doubt that his way of thinking is very different from the world's. The world says we have to have things, be on top, be filled, have it easy if we are to be happy. Christ speaks about poverty and persecution as the keys to happiness.

Obviously he approaches things differently than the world, and that is the case too, when he speaks here about peace and war.

In the passage we have quoted, Christ is speaking about the real consequences that would take place when people started to follow him. He is telling us that there is a true peace and there is a false peace. The true peace is to be found in him and in paying the price necessary to possess him; the false peace is when we put him aside in order to have peaceful coexistence with our families and fellow men.

So in this passage Christ not only repeats what is said in the one from Luke—that we cannot have him if we put something else in first place—he also tells us that in doing that consistently we are going to have a certain amount of problems with those around us who don't take kindly to our choices.

But in our fidelity to him we will find our peace.

Christ's own experience

A person convinces us more by what he does than by what he says, so it is helpful to see how Christ behaved in this regard.

Reading the gospel carefully you can see that he did not have an easy time with all his relatives. We know that at one point they were convinced he had lost it and they went out looking for him to bring him home. They must have felt quite embarrassed with his behavior to be driven to such measures.

They of course had the disadvantage of only having known the human side of Jesus all those years up to then, and they couldn't accept that he was anything else. They were probably acting in the best of faith, thinking they were doing what was best for him, saving him from himself. It does not seem the same case as the leaders of the people who later wanted him removed because they feared the Romans would come and take away their privileges.

At the same time we know that the all-important relative, Mary, did not have any part in this. Her way was always to respect the mystery of her Son, to keep the things she did not understand *in her heart.*

So we can rightly conclude that there was division in the family, and perhaps of the more lively quality. You can imagine what the others must have said against her to justify their going over her head and trying to apprehend him. And we also know that James, "the brother of the Lord," did follow him later at some stage. That, too, must have caused a stir in the extended family (he was a cousin) and perhaps even further divisions.

So Christ knows it by experience and, as always, we find that he has already walked the road ahead of us before asking us to follow.

contradictions?

And he said to them, "You have a fine way of rejecting the commandment of God, in order to keep your tradition! For Moses said, 'Honor your father and your mother'; and 'He who speaks evil of father or mother, let him surely die'; but you say, 'If a man tells his father or his mother, What you would have gained from me is Corban' (that is, given to God)—then you no longer permit him to do anything for his father or mother, thus making void the word of God through your tradition which you hand on. And many such things you do." (Mark 7:9-13)

The striking thing here is that it is the same Jesus speaking who said that if we do not hate father and mother then we are not worthy of him.

The first thing to note is that he is talking about those who use religion or religious duties as a means to shirk responsibilities. It was not that they had renounced the use of their possessions and taken upon themselves a life of poverty. Perhaps we can't quite say they were having their cake and eating it too, but certainly we can say that the cake they were meant to share they were keeping all for themselves, all the while putting on a show of service to God. It was a fine excuse and must have seemed like an all-round winner, but Jesus cuts right through it. The gurus of his day must have found his habit of calling a spade a spade extremely distressing.

The second thing to note is that in the other passages we have looked at in this chapter (and in the phrase, *let the dead bury the dead, but you come follow me*) he is speaking to those who use human allegiance to shirk responsibilities of a different order.

a question of priorities

The Church has always recognized that if a person is the only means of support for his parents, it is a sign he is not called to religious life.

Not all cases are so clear. At times you might question what exactly support means, what type of lifestyle is involved, what are your obligations as regards their debts, etc. At times there is the question of brothers and sisters who are neglecting their part of the responsibility. Even they will find conflicting duties (should they cut corners on their

children's education in order to help their parents out?...).
In such situations you have to seek the counsel of someone
you can trust, make your decision either way, and then not
look back.

different vocations

If you have very concrete duties towards your parents
that arise out of situations beyond your or their control, yet
which do not seem to conflict totally with a vocation, you
should keep in mind that there are various types of vocations
with varying characteristics. The diocesan priesthood allows
a physical closeness to your parents that a missionary vocation couldn't, for example. But you have to be very careful
and honest with yourself when taking this line of thought,
because we can very easily use it to modify rather than discover the call that God is making to us. You have to make
sure that there is a real, objective need and not (here's the
tough part) just that they find it hard to accept your vocation.

6. VOCATION AND FULFILLMENT
(MATTHEW 10:39)

*A*nd he said to them, *"Take heed, and beware of all covetousness; for a man's life does not consist in the abundance of his possessions."* (LUKE 12:15)

Whoever loses his life for my sake will gain it. (MATTHEW 10:39)

Your heavenly Father knows that you need them. Instead, seek his kingdom, and these things shall be yours as well. (LUKE 12:30b-31)

to have or to be?

To approach the question of vocation and our personal fulfillment I am going to engage in a little simplification by painting two pictures. But before writing this off, please bear in mind that the situations I describe are real, not invented, and by simplification I mean leaving aside many of the personal and subjective attenuating circumstances so that the essence of the question will stand out more starkly, rather than distorting the question or creating a non-problem.

Two couples.

One is successful and ambitious for more success. They have put off having a family because their careers do not allow them to divide their attention, because their lifestyle, if it is to continue, does not allow either of them to sacrifice career and its attendant income. Lifestyle includes their midtown apartment, constant dining out, extra long hours put into their jobs, availability to be with their clients, vacations they really need because of the high stress of both their jobs, their Lexus and their Merc.

The other couple lives in the suburbs. They already have children, and the husband was recently offered a major promotion which allowed them to toy with the idea of "moving up." They didn't do so, because there may be more children, and anyway the priority moneywise now is to put away for the kids' education (grade school, high school and college). You can tell right away in their present house that frills and luxuries are not something they go for, but once you know them you see that they do not skimp when it comes to providing opportunities for their kids: education, hobbies, music, sports…

What surfaces in these sketches are two fundamentally different ways at looking at life, and consequently two radically different sets of goals which form the background against which particular decisions (*how I will spend my time, what I will do with my raise, what place I will give money in my life…*) are made.

One life-view is centered on things, possessions, and the social status they give… This we can call the "culture of having." The other is centered on the human person, growth as a person, making each person (me and the other) a better person in himself. This is the "culture of being."

One life-view seeks to have more, the other to be more.

true individualism

Contrary to what is usually said and thought, true Christian life does more for individualism than materialism and consumerism do.

When we focus on having more, especially in our age of mass production, we are almost immediately relieved of our individuality–it is absorbed by the masses that mill around us in the mall. We want to have the same as others, or something better than our neighbor but just like someone more glamorous. We chase after the latest available product, one drop in the massive wave of consumers descending on the latest model car, or supercharged video machine, and more than ready to drop these in favor of the premium model as soon as our purse or our loan officer permits. We become anonymous statistics affecting the consumer spending index, nothing more. More often than not we do not even use the things we buy to their fullest potential; there are options that are snapped up in car showrooms which only make a difference at speeds you wouldn't want to drive at anyway—yet urged on by the relentless and fickle drums of the advertisers we become the buying slaves of their novelty.

When our emphasis is on growth, on *being* more rather than *having* more, we open in our lives the possibility of morality; for we can then think in terms of what is good and right and thus exert our mastery over things. From among the magnificent variety and quality of goods that the consumer economy provides we are then able to choose those that serve the purpose of our growth as persons, and we are also able to say no to those things that will hinder or prohibit our attaining the goals we have set for ourselves.

A person seeking to "be" more knows that not every recent blockbuster or bestseller needs to be seen or read, and some he would actually do well to avoid since they undermine his principles and his sense of morality and human integrity. And on the other hand many classics are extremely beneficial to us and we should seek them out even though no one is pushing them.

Such a person concentrates on what is important in relation to the kind of person he wants to be, on the values that make a person human, and the responsibilities he has taken upon himself (towards God and towards others). He consequently exerts more independence as regards material things and social pressure than the man whose whole focus is on having more.

happiness and self-realization

Now to go a little deeper, did you ever hear someone who has made a trip to an undeveloped country express his amazement in more or less the following terms: *I can't get over it, those people don't have anything, they live in shacks with no plumbing, and yet they seem so happy?*

It is not always true, but it does bring out a point.

In our society we have made the connection, which is false, between having and being happy. That is the principal way they have of selling things to us. Would you buy a new car if you thought it was going to bore you? So advertising makes the connection for us: buy this and with it you buy your guaranteed happiness. And we swallow it.

Things can make life easier for us. They can lighten the burden and ease the pain. They can give a certain contentment and satisfaction, especially when there is someone around to admire our possessions and envy us. But they cannot make us happy. If they could, there would be no suicides in our affluent society, at least in its upper echelons. Nor would we need to acquire more and more of them. Nor would people still seek escape in drugs.

Happiness and fulfillment are much deeper and they are directly related to our integrity, as human persons and as Christians. That is why Christ could say that the person who stood up for his faith and underwent persecution for his faith would be happy.

Happiness and fulfillment are not based then on what we have, but on what we find when we look inside ourselves and see what kind of person we are. We have a soul that will live beyond the grave. It guarantees that our subconscious will always seek realities that go beyond the grave, the riches *that thieves cannot rob and moths cannot eat,* and we will be terribly uneasy and dissatisfied if we find that all we have as persons is a few baubles subject to market fluctuations, that cannot even guarantee us the physical life and health we need to enjoy them anyway. This is why the rich and famous can have their depressions along with the rest of us.

We reach fulfillment (and true happiness) as human beings in striving honestly to be what we should be as human persons: in striving to be good, honest, moral, responsible. As Christians we reach fulfillment and happiness in striving to be what we should be as Christians, living as he would have us live, being faithful to him, and in doing what he wants us to do with our life.

However, neither human nor Christian fulfillment and happiness comes "naturally" to us though our nature clamors for both, paradoxical as this may seem.

homework

You should now be able to answer for yourself a familiar question: how could Christ possibly promise us happiness if to follow him we have to give up so much?

7. VOCATION AND THE CHURCH

(1 CORINTHIANS 12:4-30   ACTS 13:2-3)

Perhaps it is because we live in a democracy that we very easily miss the community "mystery" of the Church.

We speak a lot about community, but more often than not, in a way that primarily reflects the cooperation, order and feelings of compatibility that we have in civil society.

The mystery of community in the Church goes far beyond these, and it is even much more than the type of bond that national spirit creates—though nationalism has a quasi-mystical dimension to it, being able to rouse citizens to untold sacrifice, even of their lives, for the defense and advancement of their nation.

The Church is the Body of Christ, and we are all members of this one body. *For just as the body has many members, and all the members of the body, though many, are one body, so it is with Christ. For by one Spirit we were all baptized into one body…Now you are the body of Christ and individually members of it.* (1 CORINTHIANS 12:12-13a, 27)

Our community in the Church is the community of the parts of a body with each other. We are vital for each other, each one has to play his part well or death will swoop down on the whole body. No part of the body can take off and go it alone for then it will die …*as the branch cannot bear fruit by itself, unless it abides in the vine, neither can you, unless you abide in me.* (JOHN 15:4)

There is food for much thought here.

vocation in the Church

As a direct consequence of the above we must say that according to the New Testament our personal vocation is not an individual one in the sense that it affects only the individual involved. It affects the whole Body, because everything you do as an individual member does.

But there is something more. Your individual vocation is given to you by God in the context of the Church and at the service of the Church. Your answer to your personal vocation is going to affect, for good or ill, the whole Church and not just you personally.

So there is more to your discovery of your vocation, and your perception of what that vocation is, than your own individual feelings, interests, relationship with Christ…

While they were worshipping the Lord and fasting, the Holy Spirit said, "Set apart for me Barnabas and Saul for the work to which I have called them." Then after fasting and praying they laid their hands on them and sent them off. (ACTS 13:2-3) Here Saul and Barnabas receive their call and mission in the context of the prayer of the community. It seems their call is fruit of this prayer.

God's plan for the growth of his Body through the missionary action of St Paul was manifested in the context of the community. It was not Saul's personal agenda. Even if it were, that command of the Holy Spirit to set them aside, the laying on of hands and being sent was what mattered, not Saul's personal feelings. He said later that it was God who gave him this grace, to preach to the gentiles.

We can never find or follow our vocation well unless we are identified with the needs and mission of the Church, unless we live its life, unless we strive to be its faithful sons and daughters, unless we are prepared to serve it no matter what the personal cost or consequences.

Offhand it might seem an exercise in sophistry to say that we find our true identity as individual Christians in our condition as parts of the Church. But it is true. That is what we are, that is what God has made us by our baptism.

vocation by the Church

Set them apart. This tells us that the final word on vocation, the confirmation of a vocation, goes beyond the internal attraction that a person feels. It is an action of the Church.

This is brought out in the commitment ceremonies for every vocation because these always include the "call": the individual's name is called out by a representative of the Church (the Bishop or Superior, for example), and in response the one called declares his willingness and makes his promises, accepting the responsibilities that go with them.

vocation for the Church

Though our vocation is something God does for us, it is more than anything something he does for the Church.

It expresses not only his love for you, but also his love for his Church. He calls for the good of the Church.

This means we are called to serve and improve the Church. *Go, prophesy to my people Israel.* (AMOS 7:14) We do this by pursuing our personal holiness and by dedicating ourselves to the apostolate of building up the Church itself. We should look for what is good for the Church itself.

With no personal ambition. *And she said to him, "Command that these two sons of mine may sit, one at your right hand and one at your left, in your kingdom." But Jesus answered, "You do not know what you are asking. Are you able to drink the cup that I am to drink?" They said to him, "We are able." He said to them, "You will drink my cup, but to sit at my right hand and at my left is not mine to grant, but it is for those for whom it has been prepared by my Father"... "the Son of man came not to be served but to serve, and to give his life as a ransom for many."* (MATTHEW 20:21b-23,28)   Even the apostles felt the pull of personal ambition. John and James got their mother to press their cause for them. Peter and the rest got mad at them, because the two "sons of thunder" had tried to outmaneuver them. But the call, as Christ points out, is not for our selfish benefit. It is a call to serve, and ultimately a call to the cross. We cannot serve Christ and be at the center of our thoughts and worries.

And we are called to expand the Church. *"Go, for he is a chosen instrument of mine to carry my name before the gentiles and kings and the sons of Israel...I will show him how much he must suffer for the sake of my name."* (ACTS 9:15) This is intimately connected with the above. Only the seed that *falls into the ground and dies* will bear fruit. If it tries to *preserve its own life* it will never be more than itself. This dying to ourselves, so that it *will not be us but Christ who lives in us*, is the essential force and ingredient in the Church's missionary outreach. It has to be the essential element in the New Evangelization.

In the context of our vocation being for the Church we can call Jesus the Great Pragmatist. It is just that the fate of people is not indifferent to him. He wants them to get the Good News, and he will see to it that they do. He says to the pharisees, who have not been the faithful servants they were called to be, or given the expected fruits: *"Therefore I tell you, the kingdom of God will be taken away from you and given to a nation producing the fruits of it."* (MATTHEW 21:43)

8. VOCATION,
A PERSONAL ENCOUNTER
(JOHN 1: 35-39)

Our Catholic life is an intensely personal matter. There are certainly mass manifestations (as when the Pope draws crowds of half a million and more), but it is enough for the TV to zoom in on those faces at the moments of prayer to discover that there is a dimension to their presence and prayer that is not just communitary. We search in prayer for what God is saying to each of us individually. In other areas of our lives we may be inclined to ask what others are doing and take our lead from that, but when it has to do with our faith, with our response to God, that will just not do. We have to know what he wants of us as individuals. "What do you want *me* to do, Lord?"

The next day again John was standing with two of his disciples; and he looked at Jesus as he walked, and said, "Behold, the Lamb of God!" The two disciples heard him say this, and they followed Jesus. Jesus turned and saw them following, and said to them, "What are you looking for?" And they said to him, "Rabbi" (which means Teacher), "where are you staying?" He said to them, "Come and see." They came and saw where he was staying; and they stayed with him that day, for it was about the tenth hour. (JOHN 1:35-39)

In our job- and career-oriented world it is easy to think of a vocation solely in terms of work to be done and a role to fulfill, rather than a consequence and manifestation of the personal love we have for Christ and he has for each one of us.

the Old and the New

Scanning through the vocations of the Old Testament, the element that stands out is the call to do a certain work. God has a job that needs doing, and the prophet is called to do it, whether it be to set the people free as Moses was called to, or Joshua's mission of leading them into the promised land, or the vocations of the various other prophets to preach to the people and bring them back to the ways of their Lord. In that process the prophet encounters opposition, at times outright persecution (many of them lose their lives in the fulfillment of their mission), and so he turns to God as his only refuge.

There develops in the prophet a deep relationship with God. He goes to him to unburden himself, to seek strength, to argue, to ask what he should do, to express his frustration at the people, or his fear. But this experience and relationship with God is still dominated by the Old Testament understanding of God's absolute majesty, and the distance between him and man.

Then Christ comes and there is a radical change, for he comes as Emmanuel, God-with-us.

There is now communion and personal friendship. The fundamental experience of God in the New Testament is of a God who has come to save us from our sins by becoming one of us and dying for us on the Cross.

He is our personal savior, for he saved each one of us personally and each one of us has to accept him personally if this salvation is to become effective in us.

Interestingly enough, though John the Baptist *was more than a prophet,* and *among those born of women none is greater than John,* the gospel gives us the sense of a certain distance between him and Christ. Their paths cross, as at the baptism in the Jordan, but we don't really see them together.

John was the last of the prophets, the last embodiment of the old order. Christ for him was the *one who is to come.* He was his prophet and not his disciple. He was called to point out Christ, not to be with him, and not to spread the kingdom he inaugurated. Is this why *he who is least in the kingdom is greater than John?* (cfr. LUKE 7:28)

the personal encounter

With Christ, the mission seems to be secondary to the call, while "being with Jesus" emerges as the main element which gives sense to the mission. *And he went up into the hills, and called to him those whom he desired; and they came to him. And he appointed twelve, to be with him, and to be sent out to preach and have authority to cast out demons.* (MARK 3:13-15)   He calls each one by name.

At their first calling some of the apostles hear the words *follow me* and then moments later *I will make you*

71

fishers of men. Others hear simply the call to follow with no hint given of the future mission—as in the case, for example, of Matthew the tax collector.

We see the same experience in St. Paul. Christ came out to meet him on the road to Damascus. It was a personal encounter in which Paul received for the first time the gift of faith. It was an exclusive encounter because those who were with him only heard the voice but saw nothing: they stood by, speechless, while all this was happening, but we do not hear of any of them changing their ways in the same manner as Paul did. Paul continues that experience of Christ in prayer, and he tells us in his letter to the Galatians how he went away to Arabia for some years, which many commentators say was time of solitude, prayer and penance. No word to him for years of his mission. First he had to get to know Christ intimately in prayer. That was the most important thing.

personal call, personal love, personal mission

He said to him a third time, "Simon, son of John, do you love me?" Peter was grieved because he said to him the third time, "Do you love me?" And he said to him, "Lord, you know everything; you know that I love you." Jesus said to him, "Feed my sheep." (JOHN 21:17) Christ first verifies Peter's love for him, and then gives him his personal mission to preach and spread the kingdom.

Christ himself in the hours of his agony in Gethsemane has words that allow us to see that he lives the same order in his own life and action: he is in prayer, his human nature is rebelling against the suffering and death he sees before him, but his love for his Father brings him to say *not my will but thine be done.* In his encounter with his Father in prayer he renews his love, and in that love his human will finds reason and strength to do what his Father wants, despite the personal revulsion he experiences.

the place of the encounter

Our encounter with Christ is an encounter which takes place through the exercise of the gift of faith we received in baptism, which allows us to discover him in the eucharist and in the gospel, principally, and converse with him there, nourishing our love.

It is in this encounter, as you grow in your love for him, that you will discover the concrete thing he wants you to do. By learning to love him you will learn what he would have you do. Not that he is suddenly going to map out for you in detail your whole life; that can only be discovered one step at a time, and by taking each step he prepares you for the next. But the more we love him, the more we will think like him, and the more we will want to do what he wants.

He said some words to Peter which tell us where our concerns should lie: not in figuring everything out, wanting to know what he is asking of everyone else, but in living our own personal mission. *When Peter saw him (the disciple whom Jesus loved), he said to Jesus, "Lord, what about this man?" Jesus said to him, "If it is my will that he remain until I come, what is that to you? Follow me!"* (JOHN 21:21-22)

conclusion

We must seek Christ. Nothing else matters, and everything else falls into place when we have him. As the Holy Father repeats: *Be not afraid! Open the doors of your heart to Christ.* In prayer. In action. In charity.

9. VOCATION AND THE CROSS

(LUKE 24:13-32   LUKE 9:23-24)

It would be an inexcusable error to eliminate the Cross from Christ's life, just as it would be to neglect the Resurrection.

Both are part of the one mystery in Christ. A cross without resurrection would not be Christ's cross, and death-less resurrection is oxymoronic.

focal point of Christ's life

Two disciples lost no time in rebuilding their lives after seeing Christ, whom they had *hoped would be the one to redeem Israel*, die on the cross. They set out for home at an early hour the first day the law allowed them to travel, though their hearts were still heavy and they couldn't avoid talking about what had happened. Christ catches up with them on the road to Emmaus, and you know what happened. (LUKE 24:13-32)

When they had told him their sadness over their hopes dashed by the cross ... *he said to them, "O foolish men, and slow of heart to believe all that the prophets have spoken! Was it not necessary that the Christ should suffer these things and enter into his glory?"* And beginning with Moses and all the prophets, he interpreted to them in all the scriptures the things concerning himself.

What a lesson it must have been! And it wasn't the dry explanation of a detached academic either: *Didn't our hearts burn within us while he talked to us on the road, while he opened to us the scriptures?* they said afterwards.

Christ spoke passionately about his cross and the need for him to suffer it. It was a conviction he held deep in his heart. It was something that he knew all along and prepared himself for. It was not an accident that surprised him one day when things started to go terribly wrong. When he saw that the soldiers were in earnest he did not call upon his Father to send legions of angels to protect him from death. He had *a baptism to be baptized with,* and felt *constrained until it was accomplished.*

And John gives us the following words when Christ's human will is feeling the closeness of the moment of supreme sacrifice, *Now is my soul troubled. And what shall I say? "Father, save me from this hour?" No, for this purpose I have come to this hour. Father glorify your name.* (JOHN 12:27-28a)

Christ had long since *set his face on Jerusalem.* His cross was no surprise and no error. It was only a surprise for his disciples because they did not listen to him, and kept thinking as man thinks and not as God does when he foretold it.

a condition to follow him

During his life, Christ predicts his own passion and death, and he also predicts the cross in the life of every one of his followers.

He said to all, *If any man would come after me, let him deny himself and take up his cross daily and follow me. For whoever would save his own life will lose it; and whoever loses his life for my sake, he will save it.* (LUKE 9:23-24)

Note that Christ said this to *all* his followers, so surely it applies even more so to those who follow him more closely through a life consecrated to poverty, chastity and obedience; and in a special way to those who are identified with him in the priesthood.

Christ gives everyone sufficient warning that his way is not the easy way. *Enter by the narrow gate; for the gate is wide and the way is easy that leads to destruction, and those who enter it are many. For the gate is narrow and the way is hard that leads to life, and those who find it are few.* (MATTHEW 7:13-14)

And he also leaves us in no doubt that his cross will be our cross if we follow him; *the servant is no greater than the master, if they have persecuted me they will persecute you.*

However, paradoxically, Christ never separates the cross from hope, and life, and joy. *Blessed are you when men revile you and persecute you and utter all kinds of evil against you falsely on my account. Rejoice and be glad, for your reward is great in heaven.*

And remember, the narrow way is to be chosen because *it leads to life.*

a condition to bear fruit

Unless a grain of wheat falls into the earth and dies, it remains alone; but if it dies, it bears much fruit. Again see here the emphasis our Lord places on the positive side. His Father is a God of life, not of death. Before, he was saying how this death to ourselves is the condition for life. Here he stresses the other fruits. He has a hard time convincing us, and we resist his efforts, because we are so used to the false idea of "having life" that the world and our fallen nature teach us and seek after.

Any follower of Christ has to ask him in prayer to upend this worldly mentality we all have. Because if we do not believe in and preach Christ's message, what are we going to give the world? More of the same? There will be no conversions if we do not preach the cross, and our preaching will be sterile if we do not live the cross we preach, for we will preach with the emptiness of the pharisees who bound heavy bundles for others to carry and did not lift a finger themselves to move them.

"The blood of martyrs is the seed of Christians," is a saying that goes back to the earliest times of the Church, summing up its own experience of the fruitfulness of the cross, when the death of Christians out of fidelity to Christ did not bring about the end of the Church, but instead its extraordinary growth.

a special message for the world
When choosing to take up our cross, it is not so much that we are choosing between a life without crosses and a life with crosses, as deciding which cross to choose, or what meaning to give to the crosses that are part and parcel of our very existence. Cross and suffering are inescapable realities. It is not only Christians who have to go to the hospital, and it is not only Christians who have to bear moral sufferings, or who have to pay a price to attain their ideals.

The mystery of suffering touches every human life. Every person born on this earth has to face his own mortality.

And how he does so determines how he lives and his impositions on those around him.

Our consumer society today has set its parameters wholly within the material world, opting for its fleeting satisfactions and comforts, and the cult of the body. In the process it has bred a culture of death and egotism, a grinding and dehumanizing reduction of man to the material, where he has no greater value than a tree or snaildarter.

To save our society, to give it some hope, we are going to have to take Christ at his word, believe that his cross is the only road to life, and live and preach that, giving this same hope to everyone around us. As we search for our vocation, we should not make the mistake of looking for the wide and easy way. Even less should we commit the injustice of preaching the wide and easy way as the way of life—for it is precisely the way that has led to the despair and suicide into which our western civilization is falling.

10. VOCATION AND AGE

(1 SAMUEL 3   LUKE 2: 41-51)

When you take scripture and read it with *age and vocation* in mind, some passages especially stand out.

Samuel

This story is told in the first book of Samuel, chapter three.

Now the boy Samuel was ministering to the Lord under Eli. Samuel was young. His mother Hannah had dedicated him to the Lord from an early age, and he lived in the temple and served under Eli the priest at a time when he was very useful to the old man, who was going blind.

One night *the Lord called, "Samuel! Samuel!" and he said, "Here I am!" and ran to Eli, and said, "Here I am for you called me." But he said, "I did not call; lie down again."* Since he hadn't called him, Eli must have thought it was the boy's imagination, so he sent him back to sleep. That happened three times until finally Eli realized that there was something more at work and told Samuel what to do when next he heard the voice.

Despite his young age, God spoke to Samuel and called him. Samuel himself never thought it might be God, and neither at first did it occur to Eli. If it did he dismissed the thought in the wisdom of his years. But God insisted. If we don't read between the lines, Eli's reaction after the third call, of telling the boy what to do, seems natural and without particular merit. But, on reflection, it could not have been easy for him.

For Eli, Samuel had taken the place of his own sons who had gone astray and respected him no longer and were not faithful to Yahweh. Samuel must have been dear to him, for years before he had seen the boy's mother pray for a child, and had promised her that her prayer would be answered, and Samuel was that child. You can imagine his attachment to the boy, the care with which he educated him, and the consolation the young boy's service and righteousness was to him. But now God had intervened and Eli had to let go of this consolation and tell Samuel, basically, *I am no longer your master and teacher; listen to the Lord, do what he tells you to do.* That took a lot of letting go. He did not say, *when you have listened to the Lord, report back to me to see if you should do what he says.*

Eli acquires even greater stature in our eyes as the story goes on: he asks Samuel, *What was it that he said to you?* Samuel tells him and it was not pleasant news for Eli, it was the prophecy of God's punishment on his sons. Eli does not reject God's message because it comes through the mouth of a boy, his pupil. He says, *it is the Lord; let him do what seems good to him.*

Simeon and Anna

On the other end of the age spectrum we have two people who appear in the New Testament (LUKE 2:25-38) but are really of the Old.

God had promised Simeon that he would not die until he saw the savior, and Anna was an eighty-four-year-old prophetess. They appear briefly on the gospel scene *inspired by the Holy Spirit* to do the one thing God had prepared each one for, before again receding from our sight. They came, beheld the Child, gave their witness and then, just as completely, disappeared from the scene. It is not too much to suppose that life ended for both soon afterwards.

Mysterious, God's call and his use of his creatures.

the boy Jesus

And then there was the case of a twelve-year-old boy that confused even Mary his mother. What we usually call the "finding in the temple." (LUKE 2: 41-51)

They thought he had gotten lost by accident. Nothing so simple, however. Joseph was silent throughout. If, when the boy saw them he had run over with relief to hug them and perhaps sobbed his fright away in her arms, Mary might not have said anything either, beyond trying to console him. But they did not find him in near despair, disoriented, searching for them in tears. Instead, he was more collected than an adult, there in the temple, sitting among the doctors, listening and asking them questions; no sign of worry, fear; everything seemed to indicate that this is where he wanted to be, that it had not happened by chance.

Mary had not expected this. An accident would have been bad, but this? It apparently seemed cruel to her. *Son, why have you treated us so? Your father and I have been looking for you anxiously.* Three days of worried and harried searching, not knowing where he was nor where to look for him. It is such a natural and easy scene to relive, it has happened to all of us under some form at one time or another.

If the boy's actions were difficult to understand, his words were even more so, for his reaction was not to ask pardon. *"How is it that you sought me? Did you not know that I must be in my Father's house?"* Why were you upset? On anyone else's tongue it might have been an uppity, scathing, rebellious rebuke of an adolescent throwing down the gauntlet, enough to sever all ties and save him a trip home. That was not his intention, nor was it taken that way.

He was pointing to something they had forgotten. It is consoling when God's plans take us or our parents by surprise to realize that it happened to Mary and Joseph too.

No doubt Mary knew that at some stage Jesus would have to set out from home on his mission, and that the parting would be difficult. But she had not expected it now. In a sense they had forgotten that he was given to them, but that he was always God's, and his timetable was God's.

Or maybe they hadn't forgotten but had simply not come face to face with the practical consequences. Now they knew. The Father could ask anything of him and that was what he would do. Their place was not to question, he expected them to understand.

That gave Mary a lot to think about. As St. Luke puts it, she *kept all these things in her heart.* She often turned them over in her heart, and we see how fruitful her reflection was and how well she learned her lesson when Jesus takes up his public life; she is there in the background and at the moment

84

of the cross she is there to suffer with him. But she never intrudes. She takes her lead from him always. She had learnt the lesson: he must do his Father's business, and she must let him do it.

REAL LIFE -
MAN SPEAKS

Part II

Introduction

If it is true that God is unity and simplicity, it is just as true
that we are division and complication.

The parts of which we are made (the material and the
spiritual) instead of working together towards a common
purpose as God meant them to when he created us, now pull
apart. The weakened, shortsighted matter that we have
inherited works against the spirit, and attempts to dislodge it
from the ultimate purpose God has made it for.

If after the fall God said to Adam, "You shall earn your
bread by the sweat of your brow," in the spiritual realm it is
no less true that life is preserved and developed only at the
cost of much effort. The unity of our lives can only be
regained by effort—the cross gives life.

It should not then surprise us that, as we feel on the
one hand and agree with all that God tells us in Sacred
Scripture about our life and his calling, we should also, on
the other hand, sense a very real resistance to God's opera-

tion. *The spirit is willing but the flesh is weak*, Christ says with great empathy and insight. *Thanks, but no thanks*, is what we feel like saying.

Mother Theresa mentioned a suffering patient of hers whom she was trying to encourage by saying: *suffering is the kiss of Jesus*. From her sick bed that woman looked up at her and pleaded with disarming simplicity, *"Please tell Jesus to stop kissing me!"* We can understand her. In a way we are her. She sums up our feelings. We admire the diver but dare not walk out on the platform ourselves.

So after considering some of what Scripture has to say about the calling, let us have a closer look at some of the reasons that we never have to look for against a vocation. These and others knock on our door before we even have time to send an invitation.

1. I FEEL I'M BEING PRESSURED

Pressured by whom? How?

If it is true, you are out of the running. A seminary or religious order can't accept you! This may be surprising, but it is true. A vocation is a call from God. He calls freely because he loves you. But he calls **you.** This means all that you are. And as a human person, one of the principal things about you is that you are free. The only kind of response that God wants from you, or that is worthy of him, is a free response.

So we have to look at this carefully.

pressure and influence

It might seem at first like splitting hairs to make this distinction. But it is important to remember in the first place that we are not independent islands in the world. Our lives are affected by many people around us and by the culture we grew up and live in. As a result, we develop tastes and outlooks that become part of what we are and which, in a certain sense, define us.

All this to make a point. When talking about pressure we have to distinguish between it and influence in order to accept the reality of influence and be able to see the difference between good and bad pressure. Pressure is usually taken as "undue influence," i.e. eliminating or stomping on freedom. But it can also be "strong influence," which can be good if it does not override freedom.

The second thing to remember is that we are complex individuals. We are made up of many parts. Not only physical parts but also emotions, feelings, intelligence (usually), will, memory, appetites, instincts, ideals, hopes, spirit, sin and grace... And each one of these exerts its *influence* on the whole.

You are not an island. You have parents, relatives, friends and neighbors, groups you belong to, people who make demands on you. As if that were not enough, you know that our world is not limited to the people we see or the things we feel inside.

We live another life too, the world of the spirit, the world of the interaction—love, interest, salvation—between you and Christ. There is a further interaction—deception, seduction, undoing—that Satan is trying to establish, although he would probably blush if he had to say so in public: you see, that is his private morality and you have no right to question it.

Now, where is this leading us?

You said you think you might have a vocation but you feel you are being pressured. Well, what you have to do is sort out what you mean by that.

Is someone standing over you, waving a finger at you and saying *we have a lawyer, we have a doctor and now you are going to be "the priest of the family?"* They say it used to happen in the past, I couldn't tell. That would be obvious pressure. I've never seen it. Or rather I have seen it, but only used in the other direction: *Don't you dare go into the seminary, after all your mother and I have spent on your education...*

What is more common is for us to feel a vocation and then start questioning it. Where did it come from? Was it the Sisters in school? Am I just doing this to please my parents? It seems that I got the thought of a vocation from such and such a circumstance, from someone who mentioned it to me...*how can it be a real vocation if I could never have felt it without going on that on retreat?*...all those interminable stumpers that seem to force us to conclude, *maybe I am thinking or doing this under someone else's influence, maybe it is not a free decision.*

how "free" are we, really?

A lot depends on what we expect of ourselves. And in vocational discernment, we sometimes expect too much. We want to be totally free, and everything to be perfectly clear to us. But we are only human.

Firstly, you will never be free from influences. Advertisers will see to that. But, more fundamentally, your nature says so. It is true in the material things and it is also true in the spiritual things. The books you read will always be with you even long after you've forgotten the story. The parables you have heard from Christ in the Gospel will come back to haunt you or encourage you, depending on the direction you give to your life. The memory of good things done to you will soften your attitudes. Your choice of music will reflect your soul. If you're a westerner, you may never get to be completely comfortable with chopsticks.

Influences, then, are not an unnatural intrusion and obstacle. As a matter of fact, being part and parcel of what you are, they are something God is going to take very much into account and use when he calls you. And also his enemy the devil is going to try to use them to get you not to do what God wants. The question to ask when examining a vocation is not, *am I being influenced?* but rather, *is this the way God influences, could this be his voice?* At another time we will have to consider the way he usually speaks to us and some of the signs of his presence or influence.

Secondly, remember that how you react to the influences around you will tell you what kind of person you are. In its practical form, freedom consists fundamentally in deciding what you are going to let influence you.

As a person your freedom consists in deciding if you will accept and act under the influence of the call to the higher, nobler things, or cave in to the demands of your baser instincts that are catered to so easily in society.

As a Christian, you ask yourself whether you will live according to the influence of your faith in Christ and his message in the Gospel, or according to the world; if you will spend your life amassing only things of this world, or strive to attain those things that last beyond the grave.

The way you react to the real influences that are always there around you is what matters, not the fact that they exist.

some benefits

Thirdly, there can be something beneficial in strong influence and pressure. It can help. The pressure of competition and the fans can bring out the best in champions. The pressure of the expectations of those we respect can make us outdo ourselves. And then there are times when, despite knowing what is best for us, we know we are not able to do it on our own and we seek that support.

This brings us to another point.

the "pressure" of conscience

There are pressures within ourselves. Those that come from our conscience, causing a great number of our interior struggles. And the pressures of love, of duty, of moral imperatives.

We admire others who can resolve these inner struggles with correct actions (the hero who stands up against all odds at considerable personal risk for the sake of others). What we cannot do is imitate them peacefully.

There are times we wish we didn't know what was right so as to be able to do what is easier. Christ must understand us after spending that night in Gethsemane.

Is this pressure that our conscience exerts on us good or bad? It certainly lets us know if something is, or is likely to be wrong. It is like pain: it would be worse if we were not sensitive to it, for we'd never know the danger we were in.

But as regards conscience you have to say more. It is more like inside information: we'd never know our opportunities without it.

the "pressure" of truth

If our conscience is good for us, and its voice beneficial, what would we have to say about a real friend who respects us enough to tell us the truth about ourselves? And if the truth that he or she sees is that you might have a vocation? And if your friend argues with you? And knows when you are trying to deceive yourself? Because he tells you the truth he sees and not what you want to hear, isn't his honesty and faithfulness a form of pressure?

Often when people speak about pressure they mean this type—when an honest friend (maybe a spiritual friend or director) does not accept the cop-out and brings them up against themselves and the truth. And it really hurts when, inside, you have the suspicion the other might be right.

mature acceptance of influence

Though we are not absolutely free in the way we would often like to imagine, we are, nevertheless, free. To sum up all we have said up to now, we can say that we have intelligence and faith which allow us to examine critically all the influences we come under. Based on this examination our conscience will tell us what we should choose to do.

As long as the pressure to do the good comes only from outside ourselves we are still not mature. When it comes from inside us, or while coming from the outside it is fully accepted by us internally, then we can say that we have reached a state of maturity in the use of our freedom.

the "pressure" of love

There is something scary about the preamble, "Do you love me?"

When we hear it we know that more often than not it is a subtle set-up. Dads are wary of the question, especially if it comes from a teenage daughter eyeing the car keys. Love exerts its pressure. Love can make us do things we don't want to. Love sets many of our personal plans on end and turns our world upside down.

Yet, could we live without love? Doesn't it often make us better people, whether it be love for our parents, our country, or God?

If you love God, you are going to feel pressures that the person who doesn't, cannot. He'll laugh at you and tell you you are only on a guilt trip. Not only will your love for God "pressure" you into avoiding some things your friend thinks are normal and even healthy, it will also "pressure" you into doing other things that he will find utterly incomprehensible, such as giving your life to God to do his work.

conclusion

So I think you should look at the root of the pressure you feel. If it is from the outside and nothing more, don't give it a second thought. Don't let that be a motive for doing something as important as making a life-decision. If it starts from the outside, but really bothers you because there is something working on the inside too, if your conscience is saying *that might be right*, then it is time to do something.

It is time to go on your knees if you haven't done so yet. Because you and your Friend have a lot to talk about.

2. I WOULD PREFER TO GET MARRIED

ho wouldn't?
W Every priest and religious who has taken a vow of celibacy wouldn't.

I don't believe you.

It is hard to believe, because it is the answer to the question you asked and not the one you thought you asked. Often, when asking this question, we think we are asking: *doesn't the thought of marriage appeal to everyone?* The answer to that is, of course, *I guess it does.*

Then who could possibly prefer not to marry? Who would choose such a thing?

When our Lord told his disciples a perfectly normal thing, that a man should not divorce his wife nor the wife divorce the man, they were shocked and said that then, it was better not to marry. Christ answered, *not everyone can understand this, only those to whom the Father has given the gift.*

He took what might have been a joking, sarcastic reaction of the apostles and told us a great truth, which we are going to look at now.

the stuff of stories?

First, let us remember something all our hero stories are based on. The hero does something we all know should be done, which we should do if we were in his place and the occasion arose, and yet the odds are we wouldn't. And so we admire him when he does. As the story unfolds, we urge him on, encourage him, tell him to go ahead, pay the price, to do that noble thing. If we find that the one we expected to be a hero is no more than a coward (or no more than ourselves) our disappointment knows no telling. The betrayal stings us deeply.

Let us see what it is that is happening within us during the above process.

Firstly, we have determined in our minds that certain things have value (to rescue a kidnapped person). Secondly, we have admitted that this value is greater than others which may come more spontaneously to us (to keep my life out of danger). Thirdly, we have recognized that sacrifice is a good thing (we look with awe and reverence at the wound the rescuer received). Fourthly, there must be a proportion between the good effect (rescue) and the danger (injury or death)—you might not go into a grizzly's den to rescue a cabbage-patch doll, but what if it were a little child inside there?

But there can be something even deeper to the hero stories. Take the last question above and rephrase it, ask *what if it were your younger brother or sister inside?*

Love can make heroes of us all.

love, pain and sacrifice

Love throws a whole new light on sacrifice. It makes it explicable, understandable, right, good. We expect it.

Further still, love can possibly make us the heroes we thought we could never be. One of the most passionate lovers ever to walk this earth said that love is kind, love does not seek its own benefit, love can put up with anything, suffer anything, endure all things. *So*, he could have said, *if you want to become a hero, learn to love.*

Perhaps, though, this is not the type of love we usually think about. Generally when we think of love we think of marriage, and then only of the bliss and not of its sacrifice.

But everyone who loves encounters sacrifice, necessarily. Love entails putting someone else in first place and not ourselves—you can't do that without it hurting. That's what sacrifice is, a voluntary hurt. We can take a beating and end up black and blue playing football or ice hockey, we can slip and pay the price when climbing, we can get an abscess on a tooth; all of these bring pain, they hurt us. But there is a wealth of difference between them and sacrifice.

Sacrifice is pain willingly borne out of dedication or love. Sacrifice is what the football player does as he trains his body, when he could throw in the towel and go and party with his friends instead; when he pushes himself out of dedication to his dream: one more bench-press, one more lap, one more pull-up, even though his body is already aching and he's not quite sure he'll make first string.

Sacrifice is the mother who stays up nights by her sick child's bed; it is the worry, concern and prayer of a parent over the son or daughter away from home for the first time; it is the missionary who says good-bye to his family and leaves for a foreign land never knowing if he will be back to see them again; sacrifice is anything difficult we do because there is love in our heart.

And when we are dealing with God he gives us the possibility of turning even the unavoidable pain and suffering of life (such as sickness) into sacrifice, an act of love, by accepting it out of love for him, offering it up.

And love, when it is tested and proven in sacrifice, grows. And when love grows it accepts and embraces sacrifice more readily, more naturally.

love and imitation

There is another aspect to love, now that we are talking about it. It imitates.

Some people will go to the strangest extremes to imitate what they love, but we have all seen the more normal expressions of love's imitation, such as when we see the influence two young people in love have on one another, and more especially the young child who imitates his dad or her mother.

Love always changes us. The things or persons we love have an effect on us because they draw us to imitate the good we admire in them.

We reflect in our behavior and demeanor the things we value and the persons we value. Necessarily. We have the more superficial imitation of the kid who wears his idol on his T-shirt, and then there is the deeper, profound imitation where you change your life according to the person you love. This is what happens in a conversion.

A person is converted when he discovers how Christ has loved him, and then tries to love him back in the same way. It always means a change of life—even if you have been living well up to then. A true conversion can always be seen in one's search of the scriptures to discover the Person who has captivated us, and a search for the Eucharist to be with that Person, and a search for Penance to meet that Person afresh in reconciliation.

Like St. Paul, conversion will mean leaving what is old, what is of the world, for what is new and what is of Christ; to think like him, hope like him, love like him, pardon like him, give ourselves to our neighbor like him.

Something similar happens in authentic, deep, human love.

our original question

Are we not wandering far from our question, *why do priests not marry*, or rather, *if marriage attracts me, is it a sign I do not have a vocation?*

Not really. What we have gotten to is the core of all Christian living. Now let's see the application.

celibacy is not marrying, and a whole lot more

It is unfair to just say that priests do not marry—for this doesn't begin to scrape the surface of their promise of celibacy. If it were just a matter of an individual's personal, private choice, "his thing," with no further meaning or significance, it should not upset or offend so many people: many people do not marry and it raises no hackles. There is something different about celibacy.

It is easy for some people to realize that they do not have this call. When it is a question of choosing their state in life, generally celibacy does not upset them nor their plans for marriage. There are others who are called to this state, yet balk at the sacrifice; celibacy can be quite disturbing for them, for they are of necessity divided deeply—between satisfying or not a perfectly legitimate and human aspiration, or between following or not the call of God, depending on which side you approach their problem from.

celibacy challenges others

The celibate's unspoken message is, *this is what God has asked of me and I do it; can you do what he is asking of you as a single or married person?*

The celibacy of priests, religious and consecrated lay people is often a problem for those who are not called to it, especially for those who do not believe in the Catholic faith, because it is in the order of those heroic deeds which make everyone question himself. The challenge celibacy throws at everyone, married and unmarried alike, believer and unbeliever, is simple, direct and total—what are you looking for in life? Can you control yourself? Can you use the gifts God gives you properly?

Celibacy also calls into question their concept of happiness, the world's fascination with pleasure and, concretely today, its unbridled pursuit of the sensual.

Celibacy has to do with what we think the human person is, and what his destiny is.

celibacy challenges the priest

A priest accepts celibacy as Christ's call, in order to imitate him, and serve him, the Church and people better.

It would be good to go back over the points we made when talking about the things we are implying and when analyzing our acceptance and indeed desire for heroism to exist. We imply that some things have value—and what we are referring to here is Christ's call, the call to serve others by dedicating oneself totally, with no other distraction, to bring them the Jesus of salvation (cf. 2 CORINTHIANS 7). We also imply that some values (total service) are greater than others which come more spontaneously to us (the companionship of marriage and the fulfillment of parenthood). Such a sacrifice is a good thing (Don't we admire the martyrs who died rather than turn their back on their commitment?). And there is certainly a proportion between the sacrifice and what it gains—Christ would have given his life for even one soul.

But this is still a very poor explanation of celibacy. Viewed in this way it could still be a strait jacket, suffered grudgingly.

Celibacy especially challenges the priest to love.

love more, love more deeply

You cannot be celibate for Christ unless you are able to love passionately, love constantly, love faithfully.

Some say that celibacy is only an imposition of the Church. If it were, it might be what we referred to before as hurt. But even if we suppose it is only a harsh condition the Church imposes on those who want to be priests, and yet you accept it because you want to be Christ's priest, you have already made of it an act of love. You prefer to answer Christ's call to the priesthood in a way and with conditions that do not come easy to you. You have made an act of love. You have made a sacrifice for your love. I guarantee you, your love has taken a jump in growth. And it will continue to grow at an extraordinary rate if you are faithful to this love.

But there is a lot, lot more. Celibacy is love, and like any love, celibacy is imitation.

love in imitation

Celibacy is to choose the exact same style of life that Christ chose for himself. And Mary too. This is key when talking about celibacy.

Consecrated celibacy is to be like Christ. To want to be like Christ. To go to any measure to be like Christ. The Church has a call to be Christ, in its members, and some are called to reproduce in their lives his real virginity and celibacy.

When you consecrate your celibacy to Christ, you preach with your life. You tell people no pleasure the world can offer can compare with what it is to love him, and what it will be to be with him for eternity. And if you are ever weak, the path you have chosen will itself remind you of these things.

love in dedication

Celibacy's total consecration frees us to be totally dedicated to Christ's things. It allows a type of service and dedication that would not be possible under other circumstances.

No one better understands this than the married lay missionary. The duties of parenthood are the way to holiness for the married person and imply an investment of resources, time and energies that cannot be dedicated to the broader apostolate; the care for one another of the married couple is real and practical in its implications. For many married people, it often requires a step in faith to realize that the service they render to their spouses is of more importance in God's eyes than apostolic action that is outside their primary duties as married people. Married people wanting to do apostolate often find a first area of tension in this.

That is why St. Paul could say, *"I want you to be free from anxiety. The unmarried man is anxious about the affairs of the Lord, how to please the Lord; but the married man is anxious about the affairs of the world, how to please his wife, and his interests are divided. And the unmarried woman and the virgin are anxious about the affairs of the Lord so that they may be holy in body and spirit, but the married woman is anxious about the affairs of the world, how to please her husband. I say this for your own benefit, not to put any restraint on you, but to promote good order and unhindered devotion to the Lord."* (1 CORINTHIANS 7:32-35)

Married love and service to one another is indeed a sign of Christ's love for the Church and the way he gave himself up for it, as St. Paul himself writes to the Ephesians; *husbands, love your wives just as Christ loved the church and gave himself up for her.*

If you take that a step further, you can say that married love, because it is a reflection of Christ's love and sacrifice of himself for his Church, helps us to understand the nature of celibate dedication to Christ, which is direct imitation of Christ's exclusive and sacrificial love for the Father and souls.

So if you feel our Lord may be offering you this gift, you should take some walks on your own with him, just the two of you. He might just be proposing to you.

Don't worry, it's normal to feel a flutter of excitement as you say *YES*.

3. I AM TOO YOUNG

S trangely enough, this is an idea that, in my experience, has never come from the young person himself who feels the vocation. It is always a thought someone else puts into his mind.

Now, there can be good reasons to raise the point. Nobody wants a young kid to make a mistake, and it is important to ask the right questions. I am too young—*for what*? What kind of a factor is age? Is age the only thing that matters, does it matter at all?

Age is only one aspect, and it is important not to reduce the whole vocation question down to just age, because we have seen that in the scriptures God calls at any age.

prodigies

Although a vocation is much more than a career, it can be sometimes helpful to compare it with one, in order to understand some aspects of vocation and response.

In our world we are well used to seeing every four years a procession of younger and younger gymnasts, divers and skaters push the standards of their sport beyond what we used to think were the limits. It is strange then that we should be surprised that someone from an early age seems to know his way in life and be prepared to put in grueling dedication to excel at it. When a thirteen year old violinist takes the world by storm, we are caught up in admiration and adulation, ticket scalpers make a taking, and all we can say is "a prodigy."

To these prodigies, God has given physical and musical genius which they have cultivated with a rare blend of dedication and purpose, with the simplicity typical of childhood, to the exclusion of many other activities kids of their age find attractive and indispensable, hours of TV and junkfood among them. As a matter of fact, because of their particular gifts, you will at times even hear them refer to the interests of other kids of their age as "childish."

There are many other prodigies to whom God has given gifts of grace. They have felt the pull of a vocation from early years. They have often made options of surprising spiritual depth, simplicity and purity. At the age of twelve and in their very early teens they are prepared to do extraordinary things for God. They have a sense of and love for God that few others possess. And they can be tremendously single-minded about their goals in life.

It is easy to scoff at this. That, however, might be a mistake.

Wouldn't it make more sense to take something so beautiful, yes, and so fragile too, and preserve it, make it grow strong, make it reach its full potential? It has become somewhat of a trend to treat this as a betrayal and disservice to the young person. Is it wise, is it proper, to think like that?

I think there is a lot to consider.

What is there behind our seemingly instinctive, natural, contrary reaction to "young vocations?"

rash decisions?

There is obviously *the desire to help a young person avoid making a mistake.* His inexperience makes us want to exercise for him the caution he seems to be lacking or throwing to the winds.

We are also quite correct in sensing that he does not know practically, experientially, all that is involved in the direction he is giving to his life. He has not yet experienced in his own self the pull of ambition, his heart has not yet discovered the almost overwhelming power of attraction towards another person. There are many life-questions he has not faced—after all, *he is only a kid*, or *she's only a girl...*

How easy it is to forget that love (probably the area of life that we are most concerned about when we see a young person make the option for a vocation) is experienced as attraction and exclusion. As long as love is not exclusive it is a weaker form of love, not really true love at all.

One does not usually discover love through a process of elimination (finding out you do not love anyone else and therefore concluding that the only person left is the one you love—that would make a flattering marriage proposal!)

Actually, the process is usually the exact opposite: you fall in love and consequently you exclude everything, everyone else. That's the way it works. And if we forget that answering a vocation is primarily an exercise of (a falling in) love, we find it difficult to understand how it can be "exclusive"—excluding other options even before we know them. Just as the young man or woman in love normally does not fret over not having met everyone else in the world to be sure this is the right choice. Sure he knows there are richer and more glamorous people out there...but he is willing to give himself 110% to his chosen one and this is all that matters to either of them.

A vocation, even a younger vocation, is no different.

missing something?

There is also *the fear that he may be missing out on something.* This is very ingrained in our nature, and due also to our culture. You cannot live in our world and not be strongly inclined to think in purely materialistic terms.

By our nature we are geared towards the tangible; this is not something we have come up with recently, or of itself, an incriminating sign of decadence in our culture. What our culture today has added is the ready availability of incredible comforts and material possibilities. And it is harder to imagine giving up what you have than what you don't have. When there is so much around it is harder to see beyond it.

Our culture today, by its very abundance, absorbs us in the material, and on top of that it enmeshes us in the material by telling us directly and blatantly, as well as in countless subtle ways, that it is all that matters.

too impressionable?

And there is the concern that *he is young and impressionable, and will be influenced into something that is not right for him.*

This is rather a rash judgement about those who run the institutions for young vocations because it presumes that the young person's freedom is not going to be respected, that it will be run over roughshod. And it entirely avoids consideration of the other half of the equation: the young person will be impressionable no matter where he is, whether it be on the streets or in a high school for teenagers thinking of being priests. Where will his impressionability and his conscience be respected more? What role models will he be presented with?

Granted, for most good families, where these vocations tend to arise, it is not a question of choosing between the seminary or the streets for their child. But keep in mind that the dangers are there.

giving it serious consideration

God calls in different ways, at different times.

It goes without saying that not everyone sees his vocation early on in life. It is a gift God gives a select number for the benefit of the Church. For as the Church needs to have examples of conversion, penance and reparation, it also needs examples of the purity and totality of lives given to Christ with love from the innocence of childhood, through adolescence, youth, adulthood, maturity and persevering until the end. To have that call, and to have responded to it, makes for a very special relationship between that person and Christ. Can we deny him it?

The question parents have to face if their child is thinking in this direction is what is best for him. It is no small or easy sacrifice. God seems to pick close and dedicated families to nourish these early vocations, and it often makes the separation involved more difficult from a human perspective, and also as a spiritual sacrifice.

When the step into a high school for vocations is not the best for that individual, the parents have to renew their dedication to foster the vocation still under their roof and in their care so that it continues to grow and mature.

4. I HAVE OTHER PLANS

Depending on how you say it, this is either a flat affirmation, made to head off any discussion—the perfect wall—or a mild objection. Or it might be an agonizing realization that our ways are not his ways, much to our chagrin.

Whatever it is, it brings home to us the truth that a vocation is not of our making, while we do have a big part in following it.

When we have other plans and the vocation is wedging its way in there too, or when the order is reversed—we are almost deciding on the vocation and then other plans try to get in the way—it is very much worth our while to ask ourselves a few questions about them, their substance, their worth, and our real commitment to them.

what "plans?"

Our "other plans" come in all shapes and sizes, ranging from the specific to the vague, from the feasible to the utopian.

When we use them to stymie a vocation, we tend to emphasize their positive side and value, and our altruistic motives for preferring them. While at the moment of decision they may be presented as the most important thing in life for us, I have found that the personal plans that were the reason for not following a vocation often are abandoned afterwards at the drop of a hat. The prudent lesson to be learnt is to be a little more critical in our approach.

Define the plans that militate against your vocation, and ask yourself if you are sincerely committed to fulfilling them. What are you really prepared to do for them? Asking this question will help you see if they are something you are taking in earnest or if they are only an excuse.

This is not to say that earnest plans are a sign the vocation does not exist, but it does help us see how seriously we should look at them. You should not waste time on those that are vague and insubstantial. The earnest ones have to be treated differently.

why?

These plans, or ideas, or dreams may have come to us for a number of reasons.

A few may be authentic vocations in themselves and point to what God wants in our lives. These have to be respected.

Most are the normal hopes and desires any healthy person develops for his life as he gets to know himself and his capabilities. What they are is of secondary importance; the main question is whether they point to what God wants me to do, or if they are what he is asking me to give up in order to do what he really wants.

Some are cop-outs—when we cannot handle the reality we have in front of us we escape into a fantasy world.

Every vocation or ambition has a certain degree of fantasy to it. This is not as bad as it sounds. It is a process that starts in childhood, in which we role-play at grown-ups, and it can have very beneficial effects. It helps us dream and raise our sights.

But then there are some people who never make the adjustment to reality, applying their desire to be something better and bigger to the concrete situation in which they find themselves. Instead of having goals that are reachable, though difficult (the kid who wants that sports scholarship and is out there every day pounding the track), they live in a fantasy world, generally a world in which their dreams are totally out of proportion to what they are prepared to put into making them happen.

The Gospel tells us to be realistic in what we undertake: when you are going out on a venture—building a building—first check and see if you have the wherewithal to finish; you wouldn't want the cornerstone of the unfinished eyesore to say the folly was yours...

But we are not at the mercy of low impact dreams. We can aspire to what is noble, we can make choices that go beyond the limits set by purely human ambition or our own unaided means.

avoiding the "dream" market

Beware of the "think yourself rich" approach, whether with your other plans or with your vocation. The number of millionaires in the country is not in proportion to the number of books or tapes sold. Great things may start with the first idea or dream, but then they require dedication.

If you are thinking that our salvation and the redemption of sins is the "perfect dream," something we get for free and wonderful in itself, you're right, but that is not everything, since we have to *make up what is lacking to the passion of Christ.* Once redeemed we have to live up to it, and we need to carry our cross to do so, and to be worthy of Christ. If we do not fill our lives with good works done in grace we can expect to have *seven other spirits more evil than the first* come back to take over in our "house."

While it is healthy to be skeptical of the effortless gain-without-pain approach, we should not fall into another skepticism. We know there are things which seem impossible to us that Christ, nevertheless, asks of us. He is not expecting us to be unrealistic, but he does expect us to take into account the whole reality, remembering that *such things are impossible for man, but for God everything is possible.*

So when you have other plans ask yourself what they are, to make sure they are not just an escapist fantasy, and that you are not treating Christ's call as one either.

where from?

Some of these "other plans" are planted in our minds by others. We have all heard the story of the parent who drives the kid to be what he himself never could be, or the normal kid whose dad happens to be famous, and he spends his life trying to live up to that. However, those are the rare cases.

Sometimes they come from vague wishful thinking, and more often than not, the individual involved realizes when it is so. Sometimes they come from a realization of your talents and real possibilities. This makes them attractive and challenging, and then the individual with a vocation realizes that perhaps letting go of them is the price Christ is asking him to pay in order to come follow him.

Another very real source of our "other plans" is the world, which tells us what we should seek and how we should find our happiness. Ask yourself. Are your "other plans" worldly? Are they centered on material success only? Is their goal *to gain the whole world*? Have your soul and the souls of others entered into the picture?

their value

If you are struggling with this clash between your plans and God's possible call, it may be helpful to ask yourself which has more eternal value, the vocation God may be offering you and its fruits, or your plans and their fruits.

But the only merit of this approach is that as you make your reflection, you may hear God speaking to your heart. For you are not trying to work out what calling is best in itself, but which one is best for you because it is what God wants of you. Ask for the help of the Holy Spirit, and by doing your thinking, give him a chance to speak. That's not as paradoxical as it sounds.

5. BETTER A GOOD CHRISTIAN THAN A BAD PRIEST

Perhaps the title of this chapter sums up better than anything else the perennial temptation to mediocrity that we face. It states it in most reasonable terms, as the prudent way to go, the sure thing to do. It seems faultless.

the siren song

But in terms of the Christian life, we must say it is extremely dangerous and implies a fundamental misunderstanding of what the Kingdom of Christ is. It sounds terribly like a certain man, afraid of losing the talent his master had given him to trade with, wrapping it in a cloth...

what is "better?"

There are two main ways in which we judge if one thing is better than another: by looking at and comparing each one's value in itself, or by comparing them in relation to the job at hand. So a china cup may really be better than a tin one, but if you're packing a rucksack for a camping trip there is no doubt which you would prefer.

What we are concerned with at this point is not the theoretical examination and comparison of the married and consecrated vocations in themselves. The question here has a more practical edge to it. Our chapter could possibly be subtitled, *It's hard to be a good priest, but if I am a good Christian instead of a bad priest I will at least save myself.*

There are a few misconceptions here:
- one, the center of consideration is ourselves,
- two, it implies there exists an easy way to follow Christ,
- three, it is based on fear,
- four, it focuses on the minimal approach that concentrates on not doing evil, rather than on the immense amount of good there is to do.

no underclass

Christ has no plans for a Christian "underclass," least of all today. His Church is not made up of some who accept him wholeheartedly as Master, Lord and Friend, and then a further gray mass who don't quite.

Christ did not predict that only some of his followers would have to pick up their cross to follow him. He did not say that only some, a select group, should let their light shine before men. He did not say that loving God with all our hearts, all our souls, and all our strength, and loving our neighbor as ourselves was the exclusive commission for a reduced cadre of priests and religious in his Church.

Christ's call is sweeping. He calls all men to himself. And you are one of them.

All his followers are called to take up the cross daily. And you are one of them.

He tells all his followers they are to be light to the world. And you are one of them.

All of his followers are called to go out and preach, to give witness. And you are one of them.

Your *vocation* is the *way* he wants you to do the above.

the common denominator

Common denominators are usually bits of things. Not so with Christ. The common denominator of his followers is not a bit of them, some aspect of their lives that is similar for them all. Their common denominator is their baptism which has transformed their whole selves and consecrated them entirely to God.

the narrow way

The Christian life is a challenge, no matter what the particular path Christ has called you to live it by. The mistake of thinking that it is easier, less risky as a lay person is an attractive one—it seems to provide a way out—but it does not find any basis in the gospel or Christ's actions, or in reality.

The majority of Christians do reach salvation as lay persons, but to call theirs the "easy way" would be demeaning to them, to the price they pay for their fidelity, and to the much heroism one sees in the way they go about what Christ expects of them. Theirs is still the narrow and steep path, especially in the world we live in today, which reaches even inside their homes in its attempt to destroy and ridicule the values they live by.

No Christian was ever saved through mediocrity. *You wicked, lazy servant, you should have put it in for interest.* And the light that our Lord wants to shine before men has to be distinguishable from the darkness around it.

be not afraid

Peter walked on the waters only for so long.

His mistake was to take his eyes off the Lord who commanded him to come to him over the water, and to start looking at the waves and his own possibilities. He was caught in a paralyzing fear that stifled his faith and he began to sink. When we look at ourselves, we fall victims to fear and the power of our faith is checkmated.

Peter feared and began to sink.

The disciples feared and first they ran away, then they locked themselves up.

The rich young man feared and backpedaled. The man with the one talent feared and hid it.

Pilate feared and copped out.

Such is the pervasive presence and power of fear.

Yet, Christ insists: *Be not afraid. I have conquered the world. Fear not those who can cause you only bodily harm. I will be with you always. The Holy Spirit will give you the words you are to say. For man it is impossible, for God all things are possible.*

giving better fruits

More shall be asked from the man who received more. We have to change the emphasis in our thinking, from ourselves to Christ and to building his Kingdom. When we say something is better we tend to mean it seems more comfortable for us and suits us better. But our real focus as baptized Christians, Christ's disciples, should be on what is better for the coming of the Kingdom.

The gift of faith gives us a special experience of God's love for us. He invites us to mark our Christian living with a special effort to love him in return in the way he deserves. This includes searching and appreciating the gift he has given us. If that is a vocation, then true love for him will include making that vocation give all the fruit it can. That is really what is *better* for me.

And then for the Kingdom: with God's grace, what is the best I can do for souls? From the thoughts, reflections, spiritual sensitivity, spiritual attractions he has placed in my soul, is he inviting me to build his Kingdom through the consecrated life?

If he is, then *be not afraid*. Follow him. The spirit we have been given is not a spirit of fear but of trust.

6. MY FAMILY WILL NEVER LET ME, THEY WILL NEVER UNDERSTAND

First question: are you sure?

a true fairytale

Just a few days ago as I am writing this, a young girl spoke to me. She wanted to consecrate her life to God. Her mother understood and was delighted; the girl, let's call her Joan, was anxious to take the step; but the big problem was Daddy. When she had brought up the subject before, there had been major problems (*He has this attitude…*): no way was he going to let his daughter go anywhere, at her age, and especially if the "where" had anything religious about it. He respected his wife's decision to do religion with the kids on Sunday morning, but that was it.

But that wasn't it. You make room for Christ on a Sunday morning, and then you begin to make room for him in some prayers between the Sundays, and then you start trying to please him in what you do, and you go to ask his forgiveness when you let him down, and his help to do what he wants you to do better, and pretty soon there is something really going on between the two of you. That is how vocations often start and develop.

So she had a problem. And her Dad had one too. He had let her open the door to Christ a little, and she kept opening it wider, and now Christ was taking over. She was delighted. Dad was alarmed. She had asked him before and had just asked him again, and no way was he going to let her. Now she wasn't going to be able to do what would make her the happiest person on earth.

I knew I had to tell her to be patient. But that doesn't sit well with a sixteen-year-old. Instead of short-term answers (such as, *let's forget about the vocation* or, *run away from home to follow it*) we looked for a longer term plan—not by doubting her vocation (all the right signs were there), but by working towards it in a way that respected the obedience she still owed her father because of her age.

After our conversation, which wasn't too long, Joan went off home and I said a prayer that her vocation would in the long run be strengthened by this difficulty. The next day I got the surprise. When she walked in the door of her home the evening before, she had been asked the last question she ever expected to hear from her Dad...*Well, when are you going?*

It's not fair that others have it so easy, is it?

But there is a lesson to be learned. Are you sure they won't let you? Have you tried enough? If you feel a vocation, get advice from someone you can trust, then start working towards it, no matter what the initial difficulties are. When God calls, it all works out for the better.

who is "family?"

When there is family opposition to your vocation, the first and crucial question you should consider is: who is it that is opposed to it?

If it is your parents or one of them, then we will make some considerations further on that should help.

big brothers

But sometimes (often, in my experience) the most severe and bitter opposition comes not from parents but from brothers and sisters, especially the older ones.

At times they may be genuinely concerned, and that is touching. But occasionally when there is opposition it is because you are getting on their conscience's nerves. You are affirming priorities they would rather not think about; unwittingly you are challenging their lifestyle or choices, and you had better be wrong or stupid, because if you are not then they might be. But what are you to do? If they are genuinely fervent and practicing Catholics you can give what they say some thought. If they are not, then, basically—there must be a nice way of saying this—you have to tell them to solve their own problems before you let them have a say in fixing yours.

Don't forget either, that older brothers and especially sisters have a tendency to think of you as the perpetual baby. Don't act their mistake out. It is your life, and they cannot expect you to allow them to make your decisions for you, or take your parents' place.

parents and age

Then you have to consider your age. If you are still in high school or under legal age, then your parents or guardians have responsibilities over you that you cannot simply discount, and you have corresponding duties towards them. That is a fact. You can beg, weep, plead and insist, but if the last answer is "*NO*" there is nothing else to be done for the time being. Rather, it tells you what has to be done for the time being. You have to obey. You do not have to forget about your vocation. Just the time-frame changes a little.

But make your choices according to your vocation. Choose your friends and activities in accordance with it, go to Mass and confession in accordance with it, do some apostolic work in accordance with it, make your options as regards TV and reading in accordance with it. All of this is tremendously maturing for you.

When eventually, you do get to the seminary or formation house and find everything there helpful towards your vocation, it will be reassuring for you to know that you are not just a creature of the environment (good when the surroundings are good, woeful when they are not) but that you have some principles that you have been practicing with which you can build on.

But then you might be older, doing college, or even finishing it, and still find that your folks are dead set against your vocation. Then it is time to take some of the hard sayings of the Gospel seriously. These are the ones we tend to skim over with a vague inkling that he could not have meant exactly what he seems to say, but without being able to figure out why, in that case he did, after all, say them. And hence we skim, *if you love your...more than...*

our behavior

Let us rule out the obvious: you don't have to say to your parents, *I want to love Christ, so I am afraid I am going to have to hate you from now on.* As a matter of fact, St. John says that if we do not love the people we see, we cannot love God whom we can't see; if we say we love God and hate our fellow man we are liars. That must apply to our attitude towards our parents too.

The hinge of the matter is in the word "more." We cannot love anyone, even our closest relatives (if you marry, even your spouse), more than Christ if our love for him is going to be genuine and worthwhile. You cannot hate your parents any more than you can hate anyone else—leave that kind of foot-stomping rage for a kid going through adolescence. You are beyond that. You are in college. You want to follow your vocation. But your parents are opposed to it. And you want to know what to do.

steps to take

Firstly: do not walk away from the vocation just because it is not easy and is forcing some hard choices on you. Do not let anything come before Christ, and then deal with the situation.

Secondly: try to get to the bottom of their problem, although it may not always be possible. Why their opposition, why their fear?

- Do they object not so much to you giving yourself to God, but to the manner in which you do so (they don't want you to be a contemplative because they don't understand the vocation…they want you closer to home…they just want grandkids…).

- Are their instincts telling them something important about you that you do not see, and that might be a sign you don't really have a vocation?

- Are they simply testing your resolve?

- Are they worried and would prefer you succeed as a layman than fail as a priest?

- Are they sensitive to spiritual things or not? You may not always be able to speak to them about it, but you might be able to speak to someone they have unburdened themselves with. A helpful question to ask yourself in this case sometimes is: what would change if I told them I am going to get married and have accepted a job overseas?

Thirdly: *pray.* When we hear this advice, to pray, what usually comes to mind is prayer to God for him to change the situation and solve the problem. But there is more to prayer than that.

We usually think of prayer as asking–but it is also offering, adoring, accepting, interceding, praising. Prayer is to raise up our minds and hearts to God to know his will, to praise him for his benefits, to ask him for his grace, to look at Christ and grow in his love. Prayer is one of the means we have to transform ourselves from the weak, self-centered people we are into the type of people Christ is looking for (remember the beatitudes, the parable of the Good Samaritan).

So when we talk about praying in the situation you are now in (you are of legal age, with your parents dead set against your vocation and not seeming to take into consideration your age and decision) we are talking about *thanking* God for all the good things he has given you through your parents and for the trial you are going through, we are talking about *asking him to purify* your soul and make it strong, about offering up to him the sacrifice of not being accepted or respected, about *asking him to help* you never to waver in seeking what he wants, and about *praying for* your parents.

And how about asking him to change my parents' mind? Do that too, but don't miss the wonderful opportunity you have by limiting your prayer to just that.

Fourthly, you also need to consider your family's needs: do your parents need your support? If they do, if you are the only one they have to turn to and they are in need and will definitely need your support in the future, that is most probably where your immediate duty lies. This would in all probability rule out religious life, but depending on the particular circumstances it might not rule out a diocesan vocation. You will have to inquire.

spiritual advisor

You would do well also to speak to a spiritual advisor you trust. He will help you distinguish fact from fiction in your vocational search, and will be the second pair of eyes that will see with a little more objectivity. His insights will be enlightening, and especially he will be able to help you discover if your motives are correct. He may also be helpful in explaining things to your parents and calming some of their fears. And he will be able to give advice tailored to your particular situation.

decide

Then, finally, you will have to come to a decision. You will never go wrong if you put God in first place. It may be painful doing what you know is not understood at the moment, but if you do it to follow what God seems to be asking from you, you can do so with great hope for the future, with the absolute conviction that it is the best thing for them too.

Their acceptance may be rapid, or it may be terribly slow. Pray for them fervently. I know one priest whose mother said to me the day he was ordained a deacon, *"Now I have finally been able to accept my son's vocation."* The joy that she has now as her son celebrates Mass and she hears about the good he is doing, would never have been hers if he had not told her one day, in love and respect, that God was calling and it was best for both him and her that he answer *YES*.

7. I'M IN DEBT

I t is easy to say, *"pay it."*

the slippery slope

It is not too uncommon for a young person who has finished college and is in debt to have only a vague idea that he has to get it taken care of before he can follow a vocation. Frequently, the years just start slipping by.

debts and family

Debts are obligations we have taken upon ourselves and simply cannot run away from. But then there are debts, and debts.

Sometimes, part or most is owed to family members, and they are often more likely to take time and interest to understand your situation if you want to follow a vocation. They will probably understand that you are not looking for an easy way out, and would be the very ones to spot it if you were. In some cases their own personal situation might even allow them to pardon you part or all of your debt, but if you tend to be irresponsible this may not necessarily be a good thing.

I have also seen families rally around the young person who is setting about paying his debt. They see his goal and his willingness to work, and they pitch in—a few hours overtime here, a pinch of savings there, give up a movie and put it in the kitty, and so forth. Their sacrifices are added to and become part of his big step, their generosity becomes part of his gift to God.

Then there was another case, how unique I don't know. A young man was in debt, asked his Dad for help. He got the answer that he had better wake up and learn responsibility. A short while later he got a job at the warehouse of a friend of the family. Pretty hard work but he was surprised at how high the pay was and the opportunities for overtime which paid even better. He was able to pay off his debts and enter the seminary sooner than he expected. Only years later, when he went home for his Dad's funeral, did the family friend tell him the secret he had promised to keep: the reason he got the job and that the wages were so good was because his Dad was paying the salary, and the friend pitched in the extra for the overtime.

However, it is much more common that your family would love to help you, but there are other kids going through college now, someone else is getting his teeth fixed, a sister is getting married, a grandparent is back in hospital… Or maybe they just don't understand, or are opposed, or feel you need to get over this one yourself. Family help is out.

the cart and the horse

If asked to describe this situation, you might possibly say: *I have a debt and I have to put my vocation on hold until I get it out of the way.*

That is to put the cart before the horse.

The right way around is: *I have a vocation, so my first step has to be to get that debt out of the way in order to follow it.* Otherwise, debts tend to drag on endlessly. In other words, you have to make the decision right away, so that it is your vocation, or the possibility that you have one, that guides your actions.

Your vocation decision is not something you put off until all your debts are paid and all the obstacles are out of the way. That will be too late. Your vocation decision is what is going to put order and direction into your life and your choices, and give urgency to solving your debts.

An example might help. Jim (he is a real person, I just loaned him a new name) had some debts. Nothing extraordinary by today's standards, a few grand. He rented his own apartment, his car was old and not worth much—it was okay on gas but guzzled oil—and it cost insurance. He did not live far from his parents or from his work. He wanted to be a priest, everything else besides the debt looked positive so the advice was simple: drop the apartment and take the loss on the security deposit, move back in with your parents (they didn't mind), get rid of your car and use a bike, then cut corners, sell your stereo and some of your equipment (he was an archer and had some bows that he said were worth a lot) and in a couple of months you will be free and clear and ready to take the next step. The next time we met, imagine my surprise when he excitedly told me he had an opportunity to go to Eastern Europe... it would just take some savings he had, and a little more he was getting on loan from an uncle; no, he'd decided not to move back in with his parents; for the time being he'd rather hold on to his car and equipment. *Aren't you digging a bigger hole for yourself...?* I no longer remember his answer, or rather the reason he gave for his answer. As far as I know, years later he is still thinking of getting out of debt, his vocation still on hold.

priorities

When your priorities are not straight you can easily get sidetracked. A vocation, even the possibility of one, should be treated as a priority. It is what God has chosen for you because he loves you, and it is his plan to make your life fruitful and happy, deeply happy, in a way that the world, its ambitions and pleasures (and debts) will not.

So you have to see what is really at stake, and if you find that you are letting anything get in the way of paying off your debt, put it in its place and zero in on getting your obligation squared away. ASAP. The freedom will feel wonderful. Then you will be able to do something much more wonderful with it—you can use it to give yourself freely (and "free and clear") to God.

8. IT'S LIKE JOINING A CULT

Cults have a bad name. Jones or Koresh or whatever other leaders appear by the time you read this are rejected by society at large, and people would be quick to say that there is a world of difference between cults and so-called organized religion.

But there are some who have lingering doubts, especially when it comes to a vocation to consecrated life. Frequently, but not exclusively, these are the parents or other relatives of those young people who feel the call to leave home and country to do God's work, or who are called to a particularly demanding, "strict" form of consecrated life.

You might expect a denial of any similarity whatsoever between the two, since *cult* is such a bad word, but, as a matter of fact, the confusion is to some degree understandable. Its root is in the fact that a cult is a pseudo-religion.

A cult assumes the nature of true religion whose place it is trying to take, it demands the same total degree of adherence, and hence there is bound to be a certain similarity, though on examination it proves superficial. A cult does not have the basis to ask of its members what God has every right to ask of his followers. It is the cult that is misleading and not the contemplative or other recognized forms of consecrated and religious life.

Let us look at some valid aspects of a vocation to consecration and see how they are misappropriated by cults.

the call to faith

Faith is a grace that God places in our soul at baptism, and by it we can accept the reality of God and the presence of Christ in the Eucharist, Church and Scripture. Through faith, we can perceive his action in our souls and respond to it, we can perceive his call in our lives and answer it. We know it is he who speaks and acts through the sacraments and his intermediaries, and by faith we also can discover his action in the many signs we see around us.

This faith sustains missionaries, strengthens preachers, gives active lay Christians the certainty that no matter what the opposition or non-acceptance of the message they carry, they must persevere and live according to it and spread it.

To the person who does not have it, or who does not exercise the faith he has, faith seems like blindness, when in actual fact, it is light. It is our acceptance of God's light into our lives in order to live by it.

Anyone who forgets this, even momentarily, will have great difficulty to distinguish between the blind, pseudo-faith asked of cult members towards their leaders (or of a soldier on the battlefield towards his officers) and the motivated, luminous faith of a follower of Christ willing to make enormous sacrifices in fidelity to him.

The faith of a religious who consecrates himself to Christ is fruit of the gift given at baptism. But it is not exercised in a void. It is exercised in the context of the institutional Church, which is the great guarantor of God's action and which "tests the spirits" to see what is according to Christ. Giving yourself to Christ in a recognized religious group approved by the Church allows you to see the charism of that particular group as God's will for you. It allows you to accept the decisions of your superiors as God's will for you, and therefore strive earnestly to please Christ by carrying them out.

You obey superiors and carry out their indications, not out of any servile fear, but out of filial love of God that tries to please him as perfectly as possible in every detail of your life. You don't abdicate the use of your faculties to give yourself to God like this. If the first part of the greatest law is to love God with all our heart and all our mind and all our strength, then without our whole heart and mind and strength our service of him will not measure up. You are never asked to shut down your conscience to follow him and to obey. Perhaps here is the greatest difference between the consecrated person and the cult member. The consecrated person forms his conscience according to the Gospel, the cult member has no conscience but his guru's dictate.

Another very striking difference in this context is the search for approval that either one undertakes. One seeks it through the legitimate representatives of Christ, the other in the personal inspiration of the leader alone without reference to, and often directly against, the Church. The superiors of religious congregations and movements within the Church recognize that they are subject to the Church and its legitimate representatives. The cult leader assumes this ultimate authority for himself.

separation from home

It is true that, to be a Christian, you have to put Christ and his work above everything else, and that this is often not understood by those whose needs and wishes you are placing in second place in order to follow him.

In the past, missionaries left their families in a very real way and rarely returned to their country of origin. Considering travel conditions before the present day, we might be tempted to put this fact down to the primitive state of travel alone and not the gospel mandate, but to do so would be to forget about the many monasteries and the contemplative orders during the centuries and still existing today, where those who enter cut themselves off from family in no less total and radical a way for the sake of the gospel, even though they live in the same town.

This separation is invariably difficult, especially on the family, for they do not have the experience that the religious has of his "new family." They are full of apprehension, wondering if he will be happy or not. Sometimes the religious himself is at fault, engrossed in his own fervor and not sparing a thought for those he has left behind or, on the other extreme, burdening them unnecessarily with his own struggles and feelings of separation as he works through them to grow in his vocation.

The family, too, has to grow in the understanding of the call God has made to their child, until eventually their faith is strengthened to the degree that they can accept, support and love it. This will always be an act of faith, but again of a faith that is backed up by the Church with its approval of the different ways and charisms of consecration, each with its own characteristics in the area of contact with one's family.

And each congregation and institute of consecrated life has the difficult task of being faithful to its own God-given spirit in this point, and not seeking the understanding of men if it is at the cost of fidelity to God.

The cult demands of its members a separation and sacrifice such as is due to God alone, out of fidelity to a man and the doctrines of men. They want to be like God.

"indoctrination"

"Brainwashing" would be the not nicer way to say this. It is a real fear that stems both from many unfortunate experiences in recent years and the strange, simplistic view of man and liberty that so many have nowadays.

Nothing need be said about the known cases of cult brainwashing; there is something patently wrong there.

The deeper problem is a little more difficult to approach. People will call anything brainwashing. And the aphorism that there is no one blinder than the one who does not want to see holds true here too: to those who have already made up their minds, any attempt at teaching the truth becomes *imposition of a personal world view*; any insistence on moral standards or their objective consequences becomes *psychological coercion*; prayer, reflection are *escapism*; examination of conscience is *negative* and *creates a guilt complex*; common or community life becomes *regimentation*; a spirit of sacrifice becomes unhealthy *masochism* and *dualism*; any restraint in the use of the media becomes *fear* and *burying your head in the sand*.

The litany could be longer, but in my judgement, at the bottom of all this there is a very romantic, idealistic and simplistic idea of the human person and his liberty.

The root failing is the idea that man is of himself good, and that his greatest value and definition is freedom. We should not deny that people want to be good, like to appear as good, and often choose evil under the guise of good. But that is a far cry from admitting, as Christ in his revelation forces us to admit, that there is evil in the heart of man; that we are broken and divided persons; that our passions are active and strong and dangerous to ourselves and others; that, in other words, our ideals and dreams are one thing while our reality is another—and we need a redeemer.

If we take the simplistic idea, the path to goodness and fulfillment is easy and clear: all you have to do is act freely; anything that limits your freedom is bad; the good you do not choose "spontaneously" is no good, etc. For a person who thinks like that, life on reflection must seem pretty unfair. It is amazing how many do think that way, but at the same time accept the limitations that life in society imposes on them (all those non-smoking signs...), rebelling only when they think it is God who is moving in on their freedom.

In reality, the human person is not defined by his liberty, but rather by the *use* he makes of it. The proper use of liberty admits that we are essentially creatures of God, endowed with reason, for whom the ultimate test in our lives is to see if we are capable of giving God his place or if we will put something less worthy there, be it ourselves, our freedom or some other creature.

To shape our lives to live according to this truth, to be reminded of it, to engage in the prayer that is necessary to make it a part of us, to overcome our passions which strive to make us forget it, is not brainwashing. It is necessary if we are to grow up.

Brainwashing is based on fear, coercion, disorientation, confusion, the elimination of truly rational thought. Religious and Christian life are based on love, reflection, decision. If there is any similarity, it is in the intention and attempt to lay a foundation we can build our lives on, and which will not be shaken or compromised by the vagaries of fortune.

But the differences of method and content are so marked that any thinking person can see it is cynical and gratuitous to call what happens in the pursuit of a vocation to consecration *brainwashing*.

separation from world

The world does not like to be rejected. It does not even like to be challenged.

The idea of giving up the world and its pursuits is so strange to those immersed in it that the easiest explanation, if someone gives it up, is that he is crazy, or that he is being unduly influenced.

Even Jesus' relatives thought he was temporarily insane, and it is not unusual to hear the shocked comment of *whoever put this idea into your mind?* That it could be the working of grace, of the Holy Spirit, is not even contemplated.

Immersion in the world is seen as something healthy and good in itself. Separation as bad. As if you are not free when you are not under the influence of the world, or when you take a step back to see it in its proper perspective.

total dedication

People have difficulty at times telling the difference between dedication and fanaticism. They both seem to go beyond reason so it is easy to blunt the effect of a dedicated person (and to stifle the call to dedication) by calling him a *fanatic*.

They both seem to go beyond reason. Ergo, you have to be a fanatic to embrace celibacy for the Kingdom. Or you have to be a fanatic to base your life and life decisions on "intangibles" such as grace, Kingdom of God, love for Christ, etc.

The basis of religious dedication is reason enlightened by faith.

The basis of fanaticism is reason blinded by *the cause* and made subject to *the cause*.

Religious dedication, therefore, never oversteps the boundaries of morality, while fanaticism does so with terrifying ease.

"no time to think"

Quite a number of people would tend to agree, or at least believe if told so, that in consecrated life, above all in those groups that are more community oriented, there is very little time to yourself, hardly any time to think. And if the days are highly scheduled, as in a formation house, there is even less.

The truth is, some of the first and most important habits or abilities that you acquire in following a vocation are reflection, prayer, and knowledge of yourself, your conscience, your motivations, weaknesses and strengths. All those who follow Christ in consecrated life set aside time for prayer, recollection, retreat, examination of conscience. The religious person usually tolerates silence much better than his counterpart in the world.

The value of silence is that it can facilitate our encounter with God and with ourselves in prayer. The value of thinking, taking time to think, is that it allows us to see the truth of things, and in that way to order our decisions and actions. Daydreaming should not be mistaken for thinking.

The aim of religious discipline, silence and prayer is to discover the source of our freedom, *the truth will set you free*. It teaches you especially to use your time responsibly, to acquire habits and abilities that otherwise you might not, to value time as a gift of God for which you must give an account, and be discriminating in your use of it.

It has another very important effect: when we live under discipline, we do all the necessary and good things, although not, perhaps, at the times we would prefer. You may have to study precisely when you would like to relax, or play when you feel like reflecting, or reflect when you would rather converse. Yet you learn to get yourself to do each one despite how you feel. For someone who is to be an apostle at the service of souls, it is very necessary to be able to do this. As an apostle, your time is not your own, and you cannot afford to be controlled or dominated in any way by your whims and fancies. Besides, this is basic human maturity.

"easy to get in, not to get out"
We have all heard the stories of young people having to be rescued, kidnapped from cults, and the subsequent

deprogramming which uncovers the pressures and fears that were used to make them stay.

You are not physically locked up in consecrated life. Are you, psychologically?

The trouble with this question is not what it asks, but what it omits. It reduces the whole matter to psychological considerations and it neglects to consider that there are are others to be made—the spiritual ones, for example.

It neglects the choices the disciples had to make—as a case in point, in the gospel of John, after Jesus spoke about the gift of himself as our food and said that we had to eat his body and drink his blood to have life in us, some people turned away. He asked his apostles, *"Will you also leave me?"* There was more than psychological slavery to Peter's answer, *"To whom shall we go? You have the words of eternal life."*

It passes over scenes like that of the rich young man, the prophecies of the cross, and, ultimately, it strips all merit from the heroism that has been shown by Christian martyrs and confessors throughout the ages.

For all practical purposes, it denies that following Christ is a difficult thing, and that to be faithful to him we have to get ourselves to do things that are not the easiest or the most spontaneous.

It would deny us the happiness and fulfillment that is ours when we do overcome ourselves and discover the new, desirable dimension that moral and religious consistency give our lives—the happiness of the beatitudes.

All this to say that, if you follow a vocation to consecration, there will be times that you will feel like rebelling. And those are times that you will need the loyalty of a friend, a spiritual mentor, who will bring you back to basics. And the basics will always be: if you are called, you should see it through no matter what the cost; if you love, prove it in the times of difficulty and not only when the going is easy.

The emphasis will always be on what God wants of you. Something to be pursued in love.

9. I'M WAITING FOR A SIGN

attitude towards signs

There are two fundamentally different attitudes towards signs that we find reflected in two closely related passages of Luke's gospel.

The angel gives Zechariah the stupendous news that in his old age he will have a son who will be a prophet. But Zechariah's reaction was to ask for signs that would prove to him what he was hearing. *"Show me,"* he says. *"How shall I know this? For I am an old man, and my wife is advanced in years."* (LUKE 1:15) Trust, faith, acceptance of God's messenger were left aside. His wasn't a first case, he knew from the stories of our Old Testament that God occasionally intervened in this way, he had an angel in front of him... yet he wanted to be a little surer.

Then, later, Mary is visited by the same angel. (LUKE 1:26-38) She is given even more overwhelming news, that she is to be mother of the Messiah. Mary has a question, *"How will this be, since I know not man?"* The angel tells her how, and gives her the extra news that her cousin Elizabeth, Zechariah's wife, even in her old age has conceived and will have a son. Mary had not asked for a special sign, and when she is given it does not ask for the chance to check it out; she answers, *"Behold the handmaid of the Lord, be it done to me according to your word."* Mary asked not so much for a sign as an indication of how, concretely, God wanted her to carry out something that seemed contradictory at first sight.

These two passages can be further understood if you consider the balance you find in the following words from Matthew, which can be helpful in our pursuit of signs: *And the Pharisees and Sadducees came, and to test him they asked him to show them a sign from heaven. He answered them, "…You know how to interpret the appearance of the sky, but you cannot interpret the signs of the times. An evil and adulterous generation seeks for a sign, but no sign shall be given to it except the sign of Jonah."* (MATTHEW 16: 1-4)

Our Lord in essence told them that they had enough signs and they should not be looking for more—it is good to remember that this passage comes in the gospel right on the heels of the multiplication of the loaves.

He then says that they will be given *the sign of Jonah.* This is taken as referring to his resurrection, yet we see from the gospel that those who had rejected him during his life also rejected the evidence of his resurrection, bribing the guards to say he had not risen but that his body had been taken away by his disciples.

For a person without the proper dispositions of faith and trust in God, and willingness to accept his word, even the most compelling signs will be never be enough.

the need for signs

We do need some signs for, like Mary, we are rational creatures. God does not destroy what we are and take away our reason or our liberty in order to make us answer his call. His is an act of love and he wants our response to be an act of love too, so that it can have merit, and that means respecting our freedom.

The question of our vocation in life is not a trivial matter, there is much at stake in it—we try to find out what exactly God wants of us in life in order to do that and to be able to present abundant fruits to him at the end of our life; *behold your ten talents have gained another ten.* We know God loves us. We know he has a plan for each one of us individually. We know he is all-powerful. We know he is kind and will not play around with our lives. And, since he expects fruits from our lives, we know that he will give us enough signs and opportunity to see what he wants of us. However, these will always need and leave ample room for a free response from us; they will not take away from us the opportunity to exercise faith and trust in him.

They will be overwhelming only if we love him enough.

But there is more than one type of sign, and each type has a different function in our search for God's will.

objective signs

For comparison, take a highway sign. It shows you there are 225 miles to Boston, or that there are dangerous curves ahead. While God does not use anything as simple, straightforward, non-confusing and incontestable to tell us we definitively have a vocation, such signs do exist

153

to a degree.

They are certain unchangeable elements in your life that are just "there." More than concrete signs of a vocation we could call them preconditions for our vocation, signs that a vocation may exist, or in particular cases, signs that one does not exist. A disability that keeps you bedridden will be a sign that God does not ask you to be an active foreign missionary, no matter how much you would love to be one. The more common of this type of sign are health, particular abilities, age and obligations, in relation to the vocation you are considering.

The more general, objective signs as regards consecrated life (the conditions without which there is no vocation) are: physical and mental health, emotional health and maturity proper to your age, spiritual health, proper motivations, sufficient intelligence. Each religious group will have its own set of standards drawn from its own particular charism and apostolate, and this will show you with relative clarity if you are not called to a particular group.

We can say that these objective signs are negative in the sense that they cannot tell us if we do have a vocation, but when they say we don't they are correct.

subjective signs

We can be well excused for feeling a little wary of the category of subjective signs. We do not want to be weird or victims of our imagination. But the vocation is a personal call, and certain things are going to strike the person who has a vocation differently to the person who doesn't. You should watch out for these things that convey a special meaning to you.

coincidences

When coincidences are considered under the light of faith we can discover God's providence in them.

Material coincidences are, for example, the people I meet, the places I happen across and so forth. Our life is a tapestry of these coincidences. Friendships, business opportunities, marriages and vocations can all to a great degree point to a material coincidence in their origin: being at the right place at the right time. For one who believes that God is a providential Father it is easy to see his guiding hand in much of what would otherwise appear to be a chance happening—such as repeatedly running across the same people or group. *Are not two sparrows sold for a farthing? And not one of them will fall to the ground without your Father's will.*

Spiritual coincidences are when I keep running into similar spiritual experiences and reactions in given circumstances. St. Ignatius noticed that when he read lives of the saints he was inflamed with a desire to do the same and it gave him peace, but when he read novels the results were different, and that fact helped him to see what God was leading him to. You can receive very strong indications of where God is leading you from these experiences in prayer, especially if their emotional content is contained and not predominant. Look at what gives you peace, hope and joy in prayer, and make sure you are connected to reality as you assess your reactions (if you cannot stay in the state of grace, yet at times find yourself carried away by transports of extreme fervor, that is nice, but you know where you have to start).

Look at *your reactions* not only when you are at prayer, but also in other circumstances such as when you hear others speak about their mission, when you listen to what the Pope says on a Youth Day, when you help someone, or when you see the problems your friends get into. All of these can have meaning and make you sensitive to the action of the Holy Spirit in your life.

Another point to consider here are the *differences you notice* between yourself and your friends and siblings. Look at your values and priorities, your interests, what you find satisfying, worthwhile and fulfilling. What you tend to think about, the spin you give to things, what moves you. Your friends may be good people, but when you speak with them and discover these differences, you can more easily sense the path by which God may be leading you.

cultivating the supernatural signs

We are not talking here of seeking special revelations or angelic messages. What we are talking about is giving God a chance.

When considering what I called *subjective signs* (discovered in the providential coincidences our life is full of) we saw how they can reveal God's action already present in our souls; *No one can come to me unless the Father call him.* What we are now referring to is us doing our part to cultivate that.

There are three elements involved here and, since they are done under the influence of grace and in order to make your soul more responsive to grace, we are calling this active stage the cultivation of supernatural signs.

Cultivate an *active life of prayer* so that God's grace can enlighten your mind more freely through the greater exercise of your faith. This will help you to base your decisions on faith rather than blind, unenlightened reason.

Cultivate an *active purification of your soul* so that your passions will not present an obstacle to God's action and call.

Cultivate a more *active life of service.* Do some apostolic action so that in it God can teach you to love and sacrifice yourself for others.

As you can see, we are talking about giving their place to the theological virtues (faith, hope, charity) which will allow God to show himself to us more freely.

some extremes

One extreme when seeking signs is to take everything as a sign, indiscriminately. The smallest thing, the minutest experience is given unjustified importance. The incidental, comforting, and totally subjective is given the mantle of special revelation. This inevitably leads to confusion because it does not allow us to take things in their context, and does not allow us to give them their relative importance. A subjective reaction is put on a par with a truth of faith and sometimes above it. This hamstrings our faith because it eliminates all critical use of our reason—and remember, grace builds on nature, faith enlightens but does not contradict reason.

Another extreme is when no sign is enough. *If they do not believe Moses and the Prophets they will not believe even if someone rises from the dead.* This attitude is totally lacking in trust. There is never enough to go on, there is always reason to doubt. This person never quite trusts his spiritual director, and possibly has several he consults.

It may seem strange to have a third extreme, but frequently there is also the case of those who are decided or deciding, and do not know what meaning to give to the difficulties they experience. They take their difficulties as countersigns. Signs against. As if a vocation consisted in a calling not to have difficulties.

This often happens when our love is not strong, when we do not love with passion what God wants from us. Instead of identification between our will and his, there is distance. Love makes us strong and keeps us persevering in adversity. But love grows and deepens in trial. Very often it takes the help of a prudent spiritual director in order to help us see if the difficulties are signs pointing in another direction or if they are no more than normal, purifying trials.

10. I'M DISCERNING

Seeking signs is often connected with discernment, but seeing that quite often one can plead discernment so as to put off action, it is worth consideration apart.

place of discernment

Discernment is necessary, because without it our actions would not have the consistency reason can give them.

Discernment must take place in a climate of faith. It is the perception of God's action and his call. I believe discernment is, in itself, a grace. It is definitely more than a fruit of mere intellectual examination and reflection.

Discernment is, therefore, more subject to the pattern of grace than to the laws of pure reason. For example, God can in one moment enlighten a soul and let him see his call, much like a person can receive the grace of faith from one moment to the next with no apparent natural explanation. People can study the Catholic faith for years, argue with the best of theologians, and still not believe; then in a visit to a church, God can do in a moment what that man had been fruitlessly seeking for years. Discernment is not always a laborious process grinding to inevitable results. Sometimes it is a flash of recognition, which we test, but we know it is true.

It is extremely important to remember that while discernment is an act of the mind it is principally a fruit of grace.

Discernment should be a prelude to action. Of itself we should say it has no value unless it leads to action: *not everyone who says, Lord, Lord, will enter the kingdom; but only he who does the Father's will.* Endless dawdling will only waste the precious time you have to serve God.

discernment is not enough

If our vocational search is focused solely on discernment, the final result may be in jeopardy. If we think that once we discern our vocation there will be no more problems, we are deceived. The interesting part comes after we have discerned, and this is where the whole challenge is.

more important than discernment

If you are searching out your vocation, I would say that the least of your worries should be discernment. It does not take much faith or common sense to conclude that if God wants you to do something he is going to let you know. Give him the opportunity to speak to you and he will, eventually. Or rather, you will eventually hear him.

The important question is *will you heed him, will you do what he wants, will you do what you hear?*

the real task at hand

It is much more important to *prepare* yourself for your vocation than to *discern* it. God can give you in a flash the awareness you need in order to see it. But what happens then? Will that knowledge remain sterile?

Following your vocation requires your cooperation. It requires strength and stability of character; it requires generosity, the ability to sacrifice. It requires perseverance and overcoming the other attractions that pull at our hearts. You have to learn to love others more than yourself, and to be open to the needs of others and of the Church. You have to go out of yourself and see beyond yourself.

All of these are difficult discipline, but they are things you can and need to start on right now so that *when God's light comes you will be ready to say yes.*

Most importantly, when you are in the right disposition and not afraid of the call, you will be able to see it more easily, your discernment is more likely to be successful.

So we have to cultivate the right dispositions, no longer be afraid of what God might call us to, but tell him he can ask anything of us and we will do it.

Once we tell him this sincerely, it often happens that discernment comes much more easily, almost as a matter of course, for we can see more easily our human respect, our fears, our vanities. It is not unusual to discover that we were tending towards the right thing but for the wrong motives, or that our struggle was not really one of discernment but of generosity.

There is nothing like the peace that comes from seeking first the Kingdom of God.

11. WHAT IS NEEDED ARE CATHOLIC FAMILIES

One of the interesting things about this reason for thinking you haven't got a vocation is that if we say it right it brings us up against perhaps one of the most puzzling aspects of vocation decisions. Let's say it right.

"It is a very good and necessary thing to have good Catholic families, so how can there be anything wrong with doing that instead of following a vocation?"

In other words, there cannot be anything wrong with not following a vocation if what I am doing instead is something good.

Ready for some deep reflection?

First we have to get some basic things straight about *right* and *wrong*, *good* and *bad*.

absolutes and circumstances

There are some things that are of themselves absolutely wrong and bad. To gossip and slander your neighbor, for example, ruining his good name by telling lies about him is wrong and should not be done, ever.

There are other actions that are right or wrong depending on the circumstances and any sane person will deal with them accordingly. Take the action of sending a baseball through the picture-window of your neighbor's house. If the house was on fire and you threw it in order to break the glass and get in and save him he ought to be eternally grateful to you. If you did it out of spite because he beat you at tennis you could rightly expect him to come looking for your hide. If you were playing on the street, took a fast pitch right on the sweet spot and the result was a "homer"(!) right into his front parlor…you would expect him to be mad, but you'd also expect him to quiet down once you apologized and promised to do your best to pay him back.

omission

But on top of these there is another kind of wrongness, those things that are wrong by default. It's not that they are wrong in themselves; they are good, but not what they should be, or as good as they should be.

Suppose you go to a top gourmet restaurant and choose their "famous" hamburger. You naturally expect something extraordinary, yet what you get served up is more like what you would produce on your worst day at the grill at home—just a patty, a slice of onion and a dollop of ketchup on a pretty ordinary bun. You would probably call over the waiter to ask for an explanation. And even if he then cut the price to what you would pay at the local stand, you'd still feel somewhat let down and deceived; after all, this is a six-star restaurant. Yet the waiter could still say, *"Tell me what's wrong with it,"* and you might find it hard to express reasonably what you feel. But you would still know that something was wrong, or at least definitely not right.

switch

And then there are things which, though perfect in themselves, are wrong because they take the place of what should be there. Such as when you really want fish, order fish, expect fish, and yet get served meat, even if it is their best filet mignon. It's wonderful, but it's the wrong thing.

It is the case of someone who does not deliver what he is expected to, even if what he does is good in itself. There is still a defect, it's the "wrongness" of not delivering.

Now let's take it a little further.

love again

There are things we expect from those we love. Some time ago I heard of a pair of twins suing each other. It took a while to absorb that one for, besides it being over something quite trivial that you would expect to be worked out with a little patience, you would in any case expect some further flexibility between twins.

Why would it seem ridiculous for a father to complain, "Well if Mr. Smith across the road is not going to take my kids to the ballpark and can get away with it I don't see why I should have to?" Because the family relationship based on love should change things.

Love definitely does make a difference. It changes our expectations, and it changes our duties. Love makes demands like nothing else. Love gives a new content to the words: *right, wrong, better, worse.*

new context

When there is a love relationship involved, these words are no longer determined solely by the materiality of what they are applied to. Once we are beyond the area of things that are absolutely right or wrong in themselves, we have to look at a little more than the materiality of what we are talking about if we want to use the words *right* and *better*, and we have to take into consideration the expectations of love.

what is needed?

To build the Body of Christ, to spread his Kingdom in this world, Catholic families are undoubtedly needed. Yes, and a lot more. A lot more Catholic families and a lot more than Catholic families.

What is needed is for each person to find his place.

the Body, the Mystery

Perhaps the single greatest error we tend to make in considering the Church is keeping ourselves at the center. We can free ourselves from this to a great degree by referring to St. Paul's comparison of the Church to a body.

If the foot should say, "Because I am not a hand, I do not belong to the body," that would not make it any less a part of the body. And if the ear should say, "Because I am not an eye, I do not belong to the body," that would not make it any less a part of the body. If the whole body were an eye, where would be the hearing? If the whole body were an ear, where would be the sense of smell? But as it is, God arranged the organs in the body, each one of them, as he chose. (1 CORINTHIANS 12:14-18)

In God's eyes we each have a different part to play, a role he had in mind when he created and redeemed us, and when he called us. It is Christ's thought on how best we can serve the Church, and so it is an expression of his dual love—love for us in finding the "perfect spot," and love for his Church in providing for its needs and growth through our individual call (some as fathers, some as mothers, some as priests, consecrated lay persons, religious, hermits... each according to his own call).

vocation to service

Those whose vocation it is to form Catholic homes and families need the service of those whose vocation it is to consecrate their lives to the Lord. It is perhaps easiest to see their need for a priest's ministerial service—especially in the sacraments of Reconciliation and Eucharist. But they also need the prayers of contemplatives, and the witness of those who leave everything to follow him in religious life and consecrated life, who dedicate the whole of their lives, without distraction, to serving him and making his Kingdom come, serving Catholic families in many apostolates, especially education.

so, what is needed?

What is needed is for you to find what Christ has in mind for you.

12. IT'S TOO LATE

I read an article some time ago from the Catholic Digest that spoke of a man who was ordained a priest at the age of 79, and his children and grandchildren were present for the occasion. I don't know how recent the article was, for it was only a photocopy sent to me by the priest himself, and it came with a letter that reflected the depth of his joy and the youth of his spirit at his calling to the priesthood.

It was beautiful to read, and having dealt most my life with younger vocations, something quite new for me. God truly has his ways and his times, and how easy we are to establish categories to control the breath of his Spirit!

There is, however, a facet to the Spirit that we have to take into account to discuss the matter of older vocations, and it is this: the Holy Spirit is the soul of the Church and of its institutions, the inspirer of every good thing that has happened or will happen in the Church, the real approver behind what the Church accepts and approves. And the Spirit does not contradict himself.

This is very important, because in this matter of vocations at an older age there are two possible errors: one, to dismiss the vocation *because I am too old*; the other, to take the age policy of some community or other I am attracted to as unjust or a sign they are stifling the Spirit.

what is too old?

Any observer can tell you that the meaning of "old" as attached to vocations has shifted in recent decades. Whereas before someone in his late twenties was considered a "late vocation," now 30 or thereabouts seems to be the average age in many seminaries. Nevertheless, this does not stop some thirty-year-olds from thinking they are too old. I will not attempt to give a cut-off age or to say that up to a certain age you should try it—only your spiritual director can give advice that personal—but I will give a few pointers for your consideration:

- The priesthood and consecrated life are a *way of life* and not a *career*.
- Going into consecrated life or studying for the priesthood entails much more than taking a few more college credits, no matter how many, and some years of internship. It is a different type of life. A different approach. A different relationship with Christ *no matter how good and perfect everything was in your life before*.
- It entails a very specific decision to follow him and dedicate your whole life to doing his work in the service of the Church to the exclusion of everything else, which has very concrete expressions and effects.

- The chastity of a young, fervent Catholic for whom the time or circumstances are not right for marriage, for example, is very different from the celibacy of another who has given up plans for a family in order to follow a call from Christ. They will each relate very differently to members of the opposite sex. While the one will be open to or even actively cultivating an attachment to a particular person, the other will be making sure nothing and nobody interferes with the choice he has already made of giving himself totally to Christ alone.
- Similarly, their living of Christ's call to poverty will be different. And the need for prayer is far greater for the consecrated person and the priest, the obligation to pray far graver, and the consequences of not doing so further reaching.
- You therefore have to ask yourself if, with God's grace, you can adapt to this new way of living, thinking and approaching everything; this new mind-set and spirit.

policies

Many groups in the Church have "age policies" established by constitution, and you might be an older person trying to enter one but finding your age an obstacle.

Does this mean they are going against the Spirit? No. We have to say that they are following the Spirit. This can be hard to understand at first, especially if you are really attracted to that life. Actually it can be understood only in faith, for the Spirit is behind the charism of each approved group in the Church. He speaks through their rules of life.

Meanwhile, you are finding signposts.

The call, and not only for the older vocation, is often

unclear or confusing as we first perceive it, and it sometimes takes time, trial and error to gradually discover it in detail— exactly where, for example. When you come up against established and approved policies, it is a sign the Spirit will use to continue to direct you where he wants you to go. It is not enough to say, for example, "I see many older religious and priests doing great work—I'm healthy, how come they won't let me start off right now, even if I am in my fifties?" The one and only question that matters is, *how do I find God's will for me, is what I am thinking really what he wants?*

not now, Lord, not now

The other extreme of the age question is summed up by a dad who told me of his son who was graduating from high school and had bagged an enviable college scholarship: *"I can assure you that if he has a vocation it is definitely a late one."*

Seeing older men being called and becoming exemplary, effective and holy priests might tempt some who are really called earlier to put it off for a while. Or might tempt a well-meaning but over-protective parent.

From a natural point of view this might be understandable caution. It might also be an effort to soothe our conscience (I haven't said no to Christ, I just intend to say yes a little later). But what it really means is that we haven't, among other things, understood just how personal each vocation is.

It is easy to say, *"If I am called, the vocation will always be there,"* but you have to remember that we can't live "footloose and fancy free" forever. You can only be a teenager for so long. Pretty soon you are going to have to commit yourself to something (perhaps this is the essence of growing up)— studies, work, marriage…and the web of normal aspirations and commitments will, in all probability, compromise rather quickly our possibilities of following a vocation.

The best time is God's time.

And remember, you cannot put off till tomorrow the good you should do today. Tomorrow will have its own good works to do.

13. I'M STILL FIGHTING WITH SIN

There is some news for you in the Old Testament that you just have to hear. Pick it up if you like, it's in JOB chapter 7, verse 1. He speaks of battle and struggle. Doesn't that clear up a lot of things?

fighting

Here are a few more that will help us with our reflections. By all means look them up later because there are other interesting things said near where these come from, and you should always nourish your soul on God's word.

St. Paul was a man who was familiar with fighting. But he always fought for a cause, he never wanted the type of shadow boxing we sometimes go in for. He was focused, like an athlete who trains to win the race. Listen to what he says: *"I do not run aimlessly, I do not box as one beating the air, but I pummel my body and subdue it, lest after preaching to others I myself should be disqualified."* (1 CORINTHIANS 9:26-27) So he had a goal, and he was totally committed to that goal, and that commitment meant that he had to overcome some very serious opposition. And in the first line of that opposition he speaks about—his own body! His body didn't want to pay the price of serving God, he had to force it. You're probably thinking that this sounds kind of medieval. You're not the only one. I'm not going to contradict you, but if you say it is medieval you are taking the credit from St. Paul since he lived ages before that. And also St. John seemed to agree with him: *"Do not love the world or the things in the world. If any one loves the world, love for the Father is not in him. For all that is in the world, the lust of the flesh and the lust of the eyes and the pride of life, is not of the Father but is of the world."* (1 JOHN 2:15-16)

But the plot thickens.

Christ himself might actually have agreed with them, or…maybe they even got it from him! *"For whoever wishes to save his life will lose it…."* (MATTHEW 16:25)

So what St. Paul says is not just a "problem" that he had. He is pointing at something deeper and common to all followers of Christ. He does not seem to be talking about flagellation, but instead, about making the body follow orders and not give them. Our trouble is we take orders from our bodies, our bodily instincts, our spiritual instincts of pride, and we do not know how to go against them as saying yes to Christ would demand of us.

growth

St. Paul did not shirk this battle. And like all those who engage in it, he rose in the process to an enormous spiritual and human stature. He was no wild-eyed, thrashing, destructive zealot. He preached love constantly as the greatest of virtues, and then outdid his preaching with his actions. To bring the

Good News to the gentiles he endured *forty lashes minus one*, he was *beaten with rods...stoned...shipwrecked,* he braved *dangers from rivers, dangers from robbers, dangers* from his *own race, dangers from Gentiles, dangers in the city, dangers in the wilderness...in toil and hardship, through many sleepless nights, through hunger and thirst, through frequent fastings, through cold and exposure* (2 CORINTHIANS 11:24-27) and was the happiest of men in the process, the surest of men because he knew that once he had placed himself in subjection to Christ through God's grace then nothing or nobody could rob him of his love and his hope—*who shall separate us from the love of Christ...?* (ROMANS 8:35)

It is fabulously engaging to think over and over about such a man. The authenticity; the energy; the choleric, driving commitment; and then to see how he steered and controlled and mastered his explosive temperament, and pushed his body to such limits, because he loved Christ tenderly, and his Church, and each individual member. At times he might have had to upbraid his Churches, but the most that got was attention; he is at his most compelling when he appeals to the love that Christ has shown them and that they must return in kind.

You might be trying to slow me down by now, to tell me that I misunderstood your objection...that you know we will always have to fight, but the nature of your fight is different than St. Paul's, you are not fighting against sin which is outside you but sin which is inside you...in other words that you still fall into sin, and "big stuff" at that. That is why you are pretty sure that the vocation is not for you, even though at times the thought does come to you.

Well, there is a relation between the two situations, but I think your first step is going to have to be to take stock of where you are.

conscience

Here are some guidelines/questions you should sit down and answer. Give them thought. Give them time. Come back to them a few times. Maybe even use a notebook as you work through them.

First, a general question that is very fundamental: about your conscience. Does your conscience work right? In other words, is it well adjusted? Can you depend on it to give you an accurate reading of your standing before God?

Two different types of things can go wrong with your conscience: one, it can be scrupulous, like a fuzzbuster that registers everything and goes off seven times a block, everything is an alarm: every mistake is exaggerated, every fault becomes impending condemnation (extreme case, but you see what I mean); or, second, it can be lax, not registering any danger, like the fuzzbuster that whimpers and gives you a timid blink when the trooper is already leaning in the window explaining the ticket. You are not in this last extreme because your question means that sin registers. But where do you stand on the scale in between? Is it just the big, big ones that get a reaction from you or do minor ones register too?

There is a second general question that also has to do with your conscience. Your conscience needs input. It needs information, something to go by. Very often if things don't register in our conscience it is because we don't know that they should. Do you have what is called an informed conscience? Or are all your moral judgments just guesses? You can't get a good score on your SAT's by just guessing all the time, but sometimes we think we can lead perfectly good lives by guessing when it comes to right or wrong, or worse still, by following our feelings. Because we all know that if we ever did assignments on the basis of how we feel about them, it would take forever to graduate. So ask yourself, do I know the difference between what is right and what is wrong?

Now, there is a prejudice here you will have to overcome. Let's call it the "gray hang-up." We all suffer from it to a greater or lesser degree, and it has nothing to do with senior citizens.

Pressures around us have made us very sensitive people. We don't want to be perceived as simplistic or immature, or extremist, or judgmental, and the last thing we want to be accused of is seeing the world in "black and white." That is both naive and gauche today. You have to be "nuanced" and non-accusing. Because if you see some things are right and others are wrong, you imply that anyone who knowingly chooses what you see is right is a good person—and the one who knowingly chooses what you see is wrong is a bad person. And you shouldn't say things like that. Not in good company anyway.

So you have to be gray if you are not going to be pointed at. And the grayer you are (neither white nor black, but quite the opposite) the smugger you can be. If you are quite gray and unidentifiable, you might even get to be allowed to point a finger or two at the sin of not being gray.

examine

Once you have made sure your conscience is working well and is informed you should look at what it is telling you.

First, take a good look at your own standards and character. In the area of human virtue, have you set high enough standards for yourself (in your duties, studies, work…) and is your will strong enough to go for them consistently? How is your honesty and integrity? Do you have high intellectual standards? Are you content with mediocrity in your studies, in your recreational reading, in your grasp of the world and events? Do you have high moral standards? Do you just do what "everyone else" is doing?

Questions like these will give you a sense of where you stand.

Then, against the background of this information you can check your actual faults, starting with the general categories:

Is your struggle with habitual mortal sin? And is it particularly in one area or in a few?

Or have you gone beyond that and are now struggling with habitual venial sin? Is this narrowed to one area or are there several?

Once you get the general feeling of how things are between yourself and God, get a good guide for examination of conscience that will take you through the commandments and virtues and help you get a precise picture of your situation.[1] You will find that a good guide will enlighten you and help you continue to form your conscience.

admit

Or, if you prefer, *own up*. Generally it is called confession. It is pointless just to examine your life if it is not a step towards improving it. And the first improvement is to have God wash it clean. In our struggle against sin and in the continual improvement of our Christian life, the sacrament

---

[1] *for example*:
A Contemporary Adult Guide to Conscience for the Sacrament of Confession, *Fr. Richard J. Rego, STL*
© 1990 The Leaflet Missal Company
976 W. Minnehaha Ave., St. Paul, MN 55104

of reconciliation should never be conspicuous by its absence. Just like an athlete uses videos of his performance and their analysis by somebody more experienced to improve his output, so examination of conscience, confession, and spiritual direction should be considered the ideal way to progress in our spiritual life.

resolution, improvement

Examination and confession should never be brief interludes in an otherwise stagnant and unchanging life. They should be stepping stones and stages of development. Usually a good examination of conscience as well as telling you your faults will bring to light the circumstances that lead you to them: the occasions, people, places and things that are the prelude to your faulting, and at times your excuse for doing so. It can also bring us to see the good that we should be doing but aren't. Well understood, this realization is of the greatest help if you really want to progress. It shows you things you should avoid, and also hints at things you should start doing, if you are going to change for the better. But we need to make up our minds on these—and being human it helps greatly to have a regular confessor who can help us remain accountable for the good inspirations and resolutions God places in our heart.

hope

One of the most necessary virtues and attitudes to cultivate in our daily struggle is hope. It is also one of the most neglected. With God's help we *can* change. Hope gives joy and optimism and substance to our work. Hope is the key to resilience and perseverance.

as regards vocation

After all the above we can now come to some conclusions as regards the possibility of you, a sinner, being nevertheless called to serve God totally.

The fact of having to struggle with sin in and of itself does not mean as much as the nature of this struggle, and the level it takes place at. And this is where you need a prudent confessor or spiritual director to help you.

Some sins, because of their nature, can make it imprudent to attempt to follow a particular vocation. With others we might require special effort and help, but they still can be overcome. And then, to be under the influence of venial sin is not the same as to be having habitual trouble with mortal sin.

One important point to note is that if you do not recognize you are a sinner, you will never understand the need for God's grace, and that would only make you get in its way in your attempt to be an apostle.

Remember Peter in his boat after the miraculous catch? *Lord, depart from me, for I am a sinful man.* Christ, however, answered *Fear not, from now on you will be a fisher of men.*

Take heart.